Tales from Titchmarsh

A YEAR IN THE GARDEN

ALAN TITCHMARSH

HODDER & STOUGHTON

First published in Great Britain in 2011 by Hodder & Stoughton
An Hachette UK company

1

Copyright © Alan Titchmarsh 2011

A CIP catalogue record for this title is available from the British Library.

ISBN 978 1 444 72864 4
eBook ISBN 978 1 444 72865 1

Typeset in Bembo by Hewer Text UK Ltd, Edinburgh
Printed and bound in the UK by CPI Mackays, Chatham ME5 8TD

Hodder & Stoughton policy is to use papers that are natural, renew-
able and recyclable products and made from wood grown in sustain-
able forests. The logging and manufacturing processes are expected to
conform to the environmental regulations of the country of origin.

Hodder & Stoughton Ltd
338 Euston Road
London NW1 3BH

www.hodder.co.uk

Tales from Titchmarsh

A YEAR IN THE GARDEN

Also by Alan Titchmarsh

For Beth Chatto,
with love

Contents

JANUARY

FEBRUARY

MARCH

Contents

OCTOBER

NOVEMBER

DECEMBER

JANUARY

The Secret of Success

Another year gone, then. Mmm. Growing older is not something that any of us wants to admit to. Gaining experience is one thing – gaining wrinkles, aches and pains is another. Mind you, I was quite heartened this week when my 23-year-old daughter said that some of the freshers at her university told her she looked quite young for her age. She wasn't heartened at all. Indignant more like.

While not quite raging against the dying in Dylan Thomas mode, I do want to fend off those advancing years. I pretend to myself that I am just the same person who started gardening 50 years ago, and that I feel the same feelings (and a few more besides – mainly in my knees).

But I still get a thrill out of rooting a cutting, still enjoy pricking out, still feel a sense of deep satisfaction at a patch of freshly dug soil. Not that I dig a lot, except on the veg patch. And when I do, it is a few seconds before I can straighten up. But then, if I'm honest, it has always been a few seconds before I could straighten up. Digging gives most folk the odd twinge, and not just when they reach middle age. (And that's another thing: how can you know when you are middle aged until you know how long you are going to last?) I'm on shaky ground here, being unlikely to hang on for much more than a century. And by then, Lord knows what will have fallen off.

But lest this column should get too morbid I'll look on the bright side. "Gardeners," said a recent survey, "are happy people." And, aside from vine weevil and slugs, ground elder and snails, whitefly and grey mould, Japanese knotweed and marestail, I suppose we are.

We do take time to sniff the flowers, we do appreciate every new bloom that opens, and notice the play of the light on a lawn in late afternoon. We hear birds sing, even if we can't always identify them. We are more likely than most to be offended by eyesores, and more picky than most when it comes to flavour in food. "Why is it," asked a lady last week, "that Cox's Orange Pippins don't taste the way they used to? Is it the sprays?" I confessed that it could be, but had to break it to her gently that it probably had something to do with the age of her palate.

But enough of the perils of age – what are the bonuses? Learning to pace yourself for a start, which always reminds me of that rather saucy story of the two bulls in a field. "Let's jump over the fence, gallop across that field and have one of those cows," suggested the young bull. The old bull shook his head. "No," he said. "Let's open the gate, walk across the field, and have all of them."

I like to think that now I have the wisdom of age (if not the stamina), I can plan my beds and borders carefully, take ages preparing the soil, resist impulse buys at the garden centre, and be on top of my garden in a way that years ago I could only have dreamed of. Alas, it's not true. I still buy things at the garden centre I'm not sure where I will plant, still put things in the wrong place, and don't always dig in quite as much muck as I should.

But I'm getting better. I have to think that I am improving – maturing like a fine wine, rather than like a cheese and just going off or getting up people's noses. And let's face it, while there is still room for improvement I must still be young.

The secret of staying that way is to offer yourself new gardening challenges. Grow a few tricky alpines, make a new bed or border, or redesign the whole garden. Buy a new shed and rig it out with a fine set of tools and a work bench. Buy a greenhouse if you've never had one, and put in it a heated propagator where you can raise seeds of plants you've never grown before.

And, you know, the funny thing is that even writing these words makes me feel optimistic and even a tad excited. Childish, isn't it? Ah, and there you have it: the ability to remain child-ish – or childlike – whatever your age, is the secret of success as far as gardening is concerned, and probably accounts for the innate happiness spotted by that survey.

This new year will be better than the last one, the weather will be kinder, you'll master the knack of growing a plant that has always been tricky before, and your garden will look better than ever.

We have to believe that. It's what keeps us going. What keeps us fresh. What keeps us youthful. And as everyone knows, old gardeners never die, they just throw in the trowel. But not yet awhile. And, anyway, it's time I traded in the Volvo for something racier. I know you can't get many plants in the back of a Porsche, but I'm willing to try.

2006

A Day in the Life

Calming. Therapeutic. Healthy. All words that are regularly applied to gardening. Oh yeah? Well I've just come in from an hour or two of therapy and I'm a complete nervous wreck.

You see, nobody ever warns you about the little things that happen in the garden that can drive you to distraction. In themselves they are just minor irritations, but added one to another they can quickly mount up into quite a little nest of vipers.

In my case it usually starts with the kinking hosepipe. Now fortunately, at this time of year, I need only concern myself with the one I use to water the greenhouse, and there are days when so little water is needed that I can happily use a can. But you can bet your bottom dollar that if I do choose the hose it will kink and cut off the supply of water when I am at the far end of the greenhouse. This means that I have to put the hose down and go in search of the twisted bit.

If I'm sensible that is exactly what I'll do. But how often am I sensible? Not very. Almost always I tell myself that this will be the one time that I can free the hose by using what I call the whiplash effect. I flick the hosepipe in *Rawhide* fashion hoping that the motion will free the kink, allowing the pipe to extend and the water to flow once more. It doesn't work. But I have not given up yet. I now pull hard on the hosepipe, believing that brute force will dislodge it from its restriction. It does not.

What it does do is topple over the large clay flowerpot around which it has caught itself, and the fragile leaves and flowers of the plant it contains are smashed.

Steam comes out of my ears as I finally admit defeat and spend about ten seconds walking to the pipe, straightening out the kink and reminding myself that if I had done this in the first place I would now have finished the watering and the pot plant would still be in one piece.

As I leave the greenhouse I notice a piece of gravel has lodged itself underneath the door and refuses to move. I have to use a bamboo cane to push it out before the door can be shut and the costly heat prevented from escaping. The bamboo cane is broken. I now have a splinter in my finger that I can feel but cannot see. I suck it, I pick at it, but all to no avail. For the next week it will keep reminding me of its presence whenever pressure is applied to that piece of skin, but it will remain invisible.

I go off to do a different job, barrowing manure to a newly cultivated patch of soil. The wheelbarrow tyre is flat. I spend an hour repairing the puncture, half an hour of which involves locating the puncture repair outfit, and then discover that the wheel squeaks. I go for the oil can. It is empty. I spend the rest of the morning ferrying manure about and wincing at the ear-piercing noise. The cats have run for cover.

Which reminds me: I haven't walked the dogs. Three walks a day they need; first thing in the morning, a quick stretch after lunch, and another last thing at night. But this is a way of relaxing. No irritations there, surely? On a good day, yes, but you can bet anything that if I'm in a bit of a rush even Grace and Favour will play up. Favour will go AWOL in the wood, just long enough for me to be late for an appointment, or, worse still, Grace will roll in something. Why do clean, yellow

Labradors feel the need to use something left by a fox as an all-over deodorant? I now have to hose her off and dry her before taking her back in the house, and as I have not worn my wellies for the walk my feet are sodden from splashes from the hosepipe. But my trousers are alright, that is until Grace decides to shake herself dry and I now need a complete change of clothing as well.

Not to worry. At least I can have a new-laid egg for my tea. Why more folk don't keep chickens I will never understand. You can fit a few into the smallest garden and three or four will keep the average family supplied with eggs for much of the year. I raid the nest box. Good old Brenda has done it again. Two lovely brown eggs. They should be smashing with soldiers.

I notice that the drinker is empty so I carefully pop the eggs into the pocket of my Barbour and fill up a can of water for them. One of the dogs runs between my legs and I lurch sideways into the shed on which the tap is fixed. There is a muffled crunching sound. I ease open my jacket pocket and peer in at the mixture of plant labels, penknife, string, egg yolk and shell.

It has not been a good afternoon. But tomorrow I shall use a watering can, sweep the greenhouse floor, buy a can of oil, a tube of antiseptic cream and some fish for the cats, and keep the dogs on their leads while I walk them. I shall fill a small basket with straw so that the eggs can be safely ferried to the house, and only then will I discover that the chickens have gone off lay for the winter.

There's definitely a lot to be said for stamp collecting.

2000

Humble Yet Mighty

Uriah Heep is not my favourite Dickens character – "your 'umble" as he used to be known in our household when I was a nipper. And so humility, or rather false humility, became a bit of a dirty word. It was only when I started gardening in earnest that I discovered that humbleness could often be an admirable attribute.

It was a while before I noticed, mind you. I was mad on dahlias and pelargoniums in those early days – I still am, to be truthful. Strident scarlet geraniums like 'Paul Crampel' always give me a lift, but there are times when the soul craves something less obvious, something that needs to be closely examined to be fully appreciated.

Top of my list is a plant that gave me backache this autumn just gone – the snakeshead fritillary. Oh, what a flower! To see the arching stems, with their python-head-shaped flower buds, still tightly shut, pushing up through dew-laden grass in spring is to feel every year afresh the thrill of being involved with flowers and plants. The buds are almost grey at first, giving away only gradually the fact that they will be ivory white – the colour of full-cream milk – or that dusky lilac-purple. Then the chequered pattern becomes more visible. Why is it there? Why can something so natural be possessed of something so geometric?

Forget the dew that will soak your knees and get down close to the flowers to admire them intimately. Look at the square-ness of the shoulders of each bell and marvel at its construc-tion. Better still, grow a few in pots so that you can bring them indoors and onto a windowsill or table when they start to bud up.

Rashly, I ordered a thousand of them for planting in rough grass last autumn. Humble? I looked it, down on my hands and knees for hours with a trowel, dropping two or three of the funny little bulbs into each flat-bottomed hole, looking for the shrivelled hairs of the old roots to show me which way up they should go. But I'm confident that it will be worth it. I deliber-ately chose the dampest parts of the grassy paddock at the back of the barn, for these are the conditions they like best.

I kept 50 or so of them back to plant in pots. Three bulbs to a 3in clay flowerpot is about right, I put more in several larger containers, but somehow the fewer flowers that push up in each pot, the harder you look at them and the more you notice. As well as enjoying them myself, I'm confident that lots will be given away to friends who invite us round for supper in April (hint, hint).

Other humble flowers beat the frits to pole position. The primrose is, I suppose, the classic. In hedge bottoms alongside the fields that surround us, you can spot the odd flower at the back end of the year, and there is always someone ready to drop a line to the newspaper to say that the world has gone mad and the primroses never used to flower this early. They write in every year . . .

Not to worry. Nature has a great capacity for recovery and, as far as I'm concerned, the primrose can flower whenever it pleases. So, too, can the gold-laced polyanthus. These I grow in a border at the back of the greenhouse and I watch them open, along with the brassier *Primula denticulata* – the drumstick primula. I really can't disparage the drumsticks, but their gold-laced relatives ooze class without being snobbish. Each flower can be almost black, and each petal looks as though it has been painted on the rim by the Worshipful Company of Master Gilders. Provided the slugs don't get them. Ah, now I'm spoiling my reverie with practicality. But, again, you can get over this problem by growing your gold-laced polyanthus in pots. You can see them close to, once more, and you can divide and repot them each year after flowering in early summer.

But I suppose the humblest flower of all is the one that is putting in an appearance any time now – the snowdrop. Sheets of them look breathtaking in the grass beneath fruit trees in orchards, or under a single tree at the bottom of the garden.

The first I know of their presence is that worrying crunch underfoot as I detect, guiltily, the first emergence of their spiky shoots that are capable of piercing frozen snow. Gingerly retracing my steps, I know that it is now too late to traverse that particular patch of grass, and I must watch and wait for the glaucous-green shoots to push up and the pure white bells to unfurl. No full-cream milk here – just the pureness of snow.

Every year I vow to grow more of the named kinds (and there are hundreds – slow to increase in numbers, but supremely delicate in their forms and markings), but I still admire the plain old *Galanthus nivalis* and its double form that looks like a ballerina in a tutu.

Strange how so many flowers that bloom so early are the ones that you would describe as humble. But it is a good way of edging into a new year – a reminder that it is not the noisiest people or the showiest flowers that are worth taking notice of. Those who live a quieter life will often repay you many times over by getting to know them better.

[*cit*] 2008

Tomorrow's Gardeners

The lady with the pale blue hat asked: "And are your children interested in gardening?" I was attending one of those bashes worthily known as a charitable function. Strange phrase; I've always thought it could just as easily be applied to polite bodily processes. Anyway, the pale blue hat looked at me closely and was clearly anxious to hear that my two daughters, now in their teens, were avid seed sowers and cuttings takers. Alas, I was forced to disappoint her. "No, not at all. They like being out in the garden and they'll admire the flowers, but neither of them has shown the slightest inclination to get their hands dirty," I said.

She looked crestfallen and went off in search of another bite-sized sausage roll. I didn't feel at all guilty, I never have. You can't bludgeon teenage girls into developing a fascination for cross-pollination when all they want to do is hybridise with boys.

But is it possible, do you think, to engage children's active interest in gardening at an early age? Only if they start it off themselves, I reckon. Children naturally prefer animals: they move, they are cuddly and they make good pets. I've never yet met a geranium that nuzzled you under the chin, or an African violet that fell asleep in your lap. You can get children's enthusiasm up by having competitions to grow the tallest sunflower, but will the competitive instinct translate into a love of plants? It's hard for a spider plant to compete with a tarantula in the affections of a ten-year-old boy, and the ten-year-old girl will prefer a gerbil to a gerbera any day.

And yet there are some children who take to gardening with a passion. I was one of them myself. A strange child, I built my own greenhouse when most other lads of my age were kicking a football around in the street. What was it that appealed to me? Was it my grandfather's allotment, the thrill of rooting a cutting, my school teacher who sold cacti at bring-and-buy sales or the warm accent of Percy Thrower on the television? I guess, in the end, I was just born to it.

Both my grandfather and my great grandfather were gardeners. My father was a plumber and he couldn't stand gardening, on account of the fact that his father had made him do the weeding when he was very young. Perhaps if my grandfather had let my dad do something other than weeding he'd have taken to the soil, rather than the soil pipe, but I doubt it somehow.

All a parent can do, really is to put a garden in the way of a child and stand back and see if the child takes to it. If the urge does not come when the child is young, then perhaps it will emerge later in life. It is quite common for folk to discover pleasure in gardening in their thirties, and then they are often bitten hard. There's no more ardent convert than a late convert.

Children who are keen gardeners are, I think, in the minority, in spite of the market research to the contrary done by the

Royal Horticultural Society last year. Who, in their right mind, would believe that 35 per cent of children aged between four and fourteen years old rated gardening above television? That's what the survey said. I have no doubt that 35 per cent of children aged between four and fourteen who visited Wisley said they preferred gardening to television, but then you'd hardly have got them inside the gates unless they already had an interest in plants.

The survey goes on to say that 18 per cent of the children said that they wanted to take up gardening professionally. Wonderful, but it would be wrong to assume that this applies to the childhood population of Britain.

Mind you, what was impressive was that among these children was a six-year-old who could take heel cuttings of lavender. What kind of parents does this child have? Have they sent the rest of their offspring down the mines? Pay me no heed, I'm only jealous. Ask my daughters about heel cuttings and they'll think it's something you get from wearing your Dr Martens without socks.

I'm not bitter. As long as a handful of juveniles relish the pleasure that plants and gardens can bring, the British tradition of gardening will survive. And, to be fair, there is no sign of it waning. We are keener on gardening than ever. Ever more gardens open each year for the National Gardens Scheme, and garden centres are packed at weekends. With gardening in such a healthy state, I don't suppose I should worry too much about my failure to produce a couple of Gertrude Jekylls. After all, if one cook is enough in the kitchen, then one gardener is enough in the garden.

1996

Say It with Flowers

Sly folk the Victorians. They gave each other bunches of flowers that contained cryptic messages. Not written on bits of paper and stuffed in with the bunch – but messages that were signified by the blooms themselves. The language of flowers, they called it. You know the sort of thing – a red rose for true love, Canterbury bells for gratitude and honeysuckle for affection. These must have been popular, but I can't imagine there were many takers for houseleeks, which signified domestic economy (perhaps a potful warned of an imminent reduction in housekeeping money), or lobelia, which meant malevolence. Maybe that was a bunch to be left anonymously on someone's doorstep.

It struck me that all this has changed in the last 100 years and that for us today, certain flowers have assumed a quite different significance. Take the red rose. True love it might have signified once upon a time, but as soon as it was appropriated by New Labour, all that went to the wall. And anyway, no self-respecting Yorkshireman would have any truck with the red rose of Lancaster. The white rose of York stands for purity, innocence and humility, which are characteristics possessed, as everyone knows, by all Yorkshiremen.

The oak tree (or a bunch of its leaves) denoted strength when given by Albert to Victoria – now it is the emblem of the Conservative. (Well, Victoria was very fond of Benjamin Disraeli.)

Our own times have resulted in gladioli reminding us of Australia, courtesy of Dame Edna Everage, and daffodils being claimed as their own by the Welsh, though I've yet to meet a Scotsman who's been brave enough to give his true love a bunch of thistles. The Victorians considered that they implied victory, and no 21st-century Glasgow girl wants to be told she's an easy lay.

Marigolds once implied a love of nature, whereas now they are just rubber gloves. Nasturtiums denoted patriotism, but all I think of when I see them is Monet's garden at Giverny, where they scramble delightfully across the wide gravel path that stretches up to the house.

Olives now mean Italian holidays, not 'peace' as they once did, and box, which at one time denoted 'constancy', now means anything but, should yours fall prey to blight.

Some flowers, though, have meanings that are still appropriate. Take the ox-eye daisy, which once signified patience. If you've ever tried to establish a wildflower meadow containing ox-eye daisies, you'll realise that the wisdom inherent in the attribution still holds good.

Red poppies, like red roses, implied true love. But a decade after Queen Victoria died, they came to mean something altogether more poignant, found on Flanders Field. Poppies for us all, today, are for remembrance.

But there are some jollier meanings, too. Chrysanthemums imply bad taste. Pampas grass signifies that the gardener has absolutely no eye for design, and cerise petunias denote colour blindness. (I'm getting into my stride now.) 'Bishop of Llandaff' dahlias denote snobbery (in upper-crust gardens you'd think there was no other variety). And the same is true of the climbing rose 'Bobby James'.

Colour-leaved phormiums, busy Lizzies and *Photinia* 'Red Robin' say "I am common". White 'Longiflorum' lilies signify good taste, while 'Stargazer' lilies signify shopping at an unadventurous florist. A mixed bunch of spray chrysanths and carnations signifies that only the petrol filling station was open and you were desperate.

A phalaenopsis orchid in a pot signifies prudence, laziness and economy (it will last for at least three months with only occasional watering and you can buy one for under a tenner). A bunch of home-grown asparagus given as a present signifies one-upmanship, and a single rose of any colour with the base of its stem wrapped in baking foil shows that you were in a hurry.

Of course, the truth of the matter really is that giving anybody any sort of flower is a good thing, whether they come courtesy of green fingers or Interflora. And at least you can be fairly confident nowadays that the object of your affections will have no idea that white carnations mean disdain, that mint implies suspicion or that lime blossom stands for fornication.

You can happily give her a spring of mint in her Pimm's along with a slice of lime and she'll be happy as Larry and unaware of your motives. But if she rumbles that the white carnations are courtesy of Texaco, you could be in deep trouble . . .

2009

Chickens for All

Livestock have always played an important part in my garden, especially birds. In the beginning it was the native species alone that provided the interest and I still rush for the bird book at the first sign of anything not instantly identifiable. I reckon I have more LBJs in the garden than anyone else. LBJs are Little Brown Jobs, anything from grasshopper warblers to corn buntings. But there are brighter joys too, thanks to goldcrests and greenfinches, green woodpeckers and siskins.

I enjoy watching the bird population change with the seasons. The arrival of the first swallow always gives me a thrill, while the arrival of fieldfares makes me shudder; they arrive when the weather turns bleaker.

However, for the past few years there have been other birds in my garden. Birds of the non-migratory kind. In a fenced area at the top of the slope are chickens. I won't let them loose in the garden proper because I reckon that chickens and plants don't mix, except in a chicken's gizzard.

In spite of this jaundiced view, I enjoy their company, even if they are the second most stupid beings on the planet, the first most stupid are sheep and I don't have any of those. Most garden-ers would also have quite a job fitting sheep into their plots, but even in a tiny garden it is still possible to squeeze in a few chick-ens, especially if they are bantams. I wish more folk would.

All you need is a small, moveable ark that has a wire-enclosed run attached to make it foxproof: then you can move it and the chickens around the lawn. Of course, if you want to create the most idyllic setting you put the ark on rough grass under fruit trees. Move the ark around every two or three days and the birds will not only keep the grass down but they will also pluck out slugs and other garden pests to form part of their balanced diet.

I've found that four hens produce enough eggs for a family of four. Mine tend to go off lay in October and come back on lay around New Year's Day. I reckon a freshly laid egg with crisp, buttered soldiers must make the best start to anybody's day.

Over the years I've kept many chickens, all of them pure breeds. At the start, seven or eight years ago, there were grey mottled Cuckoo Marans which were a touch aggressive, but laid lovely brown eggs. Then there were the Buff Orpingtons, that looked like great globes of orange fluff and seemed to go broody at the drop of an egg and had to be shut in a draughty coop to persuade them that eggs were what I wanted, not more chickens.

I had two Light Sussex hens with lovely ivory-white bodies and contrasting black necks. There were handsome Australorps, black with an iridescent green sheen and bright red combs, and Barnevelders, hand-painted confections of brown and black. Some of these hens lasted longer than others.

Right now I have a Gold Brahma called Marjorie, who is a robust bird with feathery breeches for legs and whom my mother calls Pat, because she looks like the woman in *EastEnders*. There's one Australorp, Brenda, who's a bit of a bully, but she always gets her comeuppance from Horatio, who's a Lavender

Pekin cockerel. He stands about a foot high in his blue-grey feathers, topped off by a bright red comb, and he has two ladies of a similar hue who so far have not been named. They lay eggs about the same size as a quail which make the most lovely bright yellow omelettes, thanks to the birds being fed entirely on corn and grass.

So don't think that chickens are only for smallholders and farmers. Get hold of a book on poultry keeping that will give you the pros and cons. If you take the plunge, you will discover just how yellow scrambled eggs can be, rather than that pasty creamy-yellow colour that they are when shop-bought. Fence your chickens in well and provide them with a good grassy run and you'll have huge fun and great breakfasts. And you can't say that for your LBJs.

[*cit*] 1998

The Book Towers

Following a visit to someone's house the other day, I came away with the feeling that something was missing. It was a beautiful house, very old and very elegant. I couldn't put my finger on what was lacking for a while, but then it suddenly dawned. The house contained no books. There might have been a Harry Potter on a bedside table, or a Delia or Jamie on the kitchen worktop, but there were no book shelves. Anywhere.

Now I don't want to sound snooty, over-erudite or just plain arrogant, but I simply don't know how people can survive without books. I've had a problem with them since I was about 19. I can't stop buying them. What Imelda Marcos is to shoes, I am to books. I'm drowning in them. My study is almost untraversable because of books. The room is shelved from floor to ceiling, but books stand on the floor too in piles that are only shortened when they finally slide, Pisa-like, into an amorphous heap.

There are gardening books in the study, biographies and novels in the hall, books on natural history, sailing and British topography in the library, along with all sorts of old oddities. Clearly I have a problem, mentally as well as physically. But I love my books, either devouring them in one sitting or dipping into them for some useful nugget. Reading, I reckon, broadens the mind even more than travel.

My space problem is not helped by the numerous review copies of gardening books that arrive at the rate of one or two a week. No, I'm not moaning. It's a perk of the job and I do enjoy them. Most of them. But there comes a point when I have to have a clear out.

A friend of mine runs a second-hand book business and once a year he takes away boxloads of books. Gardeners are a prolific bunch when it comes to putting their thoughts down on paper, and I speak with more than the faintest feeling of guilt. The Titchmarsh total now stands in the mid-thirties, not counting novels, and another is about to hit the bookshops.

But what to keep and what to pass on? Tricky. Standard works must stay. They change the names of plants so often that I need to keep abreast of the current vocabulary. The authors here may not be known to me, but you can tell from the way the book is set out, and its jacket copy, if it's a reliable volume or just a doorstop. But there are certain authors who are always worth the shelf space: Beth Chatto, Anna Pavord, Christopher Lloyd and Graham Stuart Thomas, as well as several newcomers.

I am often bogged down by garden design books: small gardens, country gardens, town gardens, gardens in spaces you can't swing a cat in. But they repay a quick flip through to seek inspiration for my own garden and for *Ground Force*, so even these aren't easy to hand over to my bookshop friend.

Yet I must have a clean out. In the interests of health and safety I must have access to more carpet in my study. Some of the oldies will have to go. But who on earth could ditch Bunyard's *Old Garden Roses* or Farrer's *The English Rock-Garden*, even if the new and brilliant *Alpine Garden Society Encyclopaedia of Alpines* is now sitting alongside it in its sparkling black and gold livery?

Can I ever bring myself to dispose of an almost complete set of Collingridge *Amateur Gardening* handbooks from the 1960s, or the two-volume set of *Newnes Successful Gardening* that I bought on my first day at work? Maybe I could relinquish Walter Brett's *The Book of Garden Improvements*. Its ideas of modernity date from the 1950s and I don't see the formal rose garden making a come-back. Ah, but then sentiment comes into play. I remember looking at that book on winter nights when I was thinking about taking up gardening as a profession. That's why I still have *Percy Thrower's Encyclopaedia of Gardening*. To get rid of that would be to forget too much.

So I'm stuck with them. We could move house, but I don't know how the memsahib would react to that. Better, perhaps, than to a request for yet more shelving. Or should I just put a sign on the front door saying "Bookshop" and see what happens? Maybe later. I think if I'm careful I can make two piles out of the one tall one by the door and then it will be another couple of weeks before matters come to a head once more. And yet, procrastination is the thief of time. I know that. I read it in a book once.

2002

FEBRUARY

Taking Stock

At the start of every year I walk round the garden to take stock. It's a sort of cleansing operation – the horticultural equivalent of the US President's State of the Union address. I'll look at what's doing well and what's not, and decide on changes that need to be made.

It all sounds very organised but then, after the straightforward task of spotting the possible areas of improvement, I have to fulfil all those things on my wish list. And by the time New Year comes round, I can guarantee there'll be a good number that I never got around to.

Of course, it's all too easy to dwell on failures. Gardeners are good at that. We like challenges and feel dispirited when we don't come up to scratch. But what often comes to the fore at this time of year, as I make my perambulation, is the number of plants that do well in spite of me rather than because of me.

Now it's here that I have to exercise self-control. You see, there's a streak in all of us that rather resents plants deciding where they will grow. Surely it is the gardener who places them? If plants are left to their own devices, they can ruin an otherwise carefully crafted landscape. Leave self-distribution unchecked and before we know where we are, we'd lose control completely and the whole garden would be overrun with aliens, wouldn't it?

Well, yes, to a point. But I rather enjoy a helping hand in my garden when it comes to layout, and sometimes happy chances give a garden a sense of exuberance that total control in planting stifles.

Is this beginning to sound like an excuse for a *laissez-faire* attitude? Well, what the heck. I regard it as my plants' way of telling me what they like and where they like it and, as we all know that the key to good gardening is "right plant, right place", it seems churlish to argue with those plants that are prepared to tell you exactly what they want and where.

But this does not stop us from despising "good doers". I have, in my time, been very scathing of plants that are nothing more than thugs. I will still not plant variegated ground elder. I had it in the garden at Barleywood and it romped over a patch of ground underneath a flat-branched viburnum. "It's not as invasive as the common green sort," they'll tell you, in the same way they'll say Mussolini was not as bad as Hitler.

But lady's mantle? Ah, dear old *Alchemilla mollis*. Of course, she's every bit as likely to colonise a lump of border the size of a football pitch as is ground elder, but she has finer attributes – softly downy scalloped leaves, which hold water droplets like orbs of quicksilver, and those frothy lime-green flowers that are wonderful for bulking out flower arrangements.

No, lady's mantle stays and I dig out the lumps I don't want and shear off the flowers before they set seed. And, bless her, she makes great ground cover in dappled shade. Sorted. And Bowles's golden grass (*Milium effusum* 'Aureum')? Again, it seeds itself a little too freely, but is easy enough to yank out where it's not wanted. I have it sprinkled through a plantation of purple and gold plants – berberis and heuchera, weigela and robinia – not a subtle mixture, but one that makes me smile.

Ranking with alchemilla in my affections is the purple cow parsley *Anthriscus sylvestris* 'Ravenswing'. It seeds itself through this purple and gold section quite happily and, like many ornamental grasses, is useful 'glue' in a border of individuals, giving cohesion to an otherwise bitty part of the garden where I want to try lots of different plants – not necessarily in threes and fives. But it does seed itself just a little too generously, and while generally coming true from seed, you will find individuals that are green or veering in that direction. You'll need to prise out offenders with a long-bladed trowel, making sure the tap root comes too, leaving only the deepest purple progeny behind.

Aquilegias I do have to watch. They seed themselves everywhere and the flowers can become smaller and muddier if they are left to interbreed willy-nilly. The only way to solve the aquilegia problem is to be hard-hearted at flowering time and pull out any plants whose blooms are less than captivating. It's a tough moment, but you'll be glad you bit the bullet.

Every gardener will have a different opinion about plants whose energy and willingness to please can make them a problem. I find it hard to discourage Miss Willmott's Ghost (*Eryngium giganteum*), which now happily pops up all along a border underneath three clumps of silver birch (rather fitting that) and the lovely white-flowered *Omphalodes linifolia* – an annual that never moves far, and whose common name of Venus's navelwort ensures her a place in my affections.

But then there are the celandines, the polemoniums, the geraniums and forget-me-nots. Everything in moderation but ... Where's my list?

2009

Dreaming of Summer

Cold nights. Long, cold nights. Nights when I gaze at the smouldering logs in the fire. Each shower of sparks that spirals up the chimney ignites another memory of the summer past. Ah, yes, winter is a time to daydream. Gardeners like to look forward, but I like to look back, too, and savour the memories of warm summer days now long gone. So what do I remember of the summer of 96? Not as long and hot as 95, but none the worse for that. Though there was still not a hose-pipe in sight in Yorkshire, not until last November anyway.

As I gaze at the licking flames of the roaring fire, I can see the scarlet nasturtiums that tumbled from a terracotta pot, like chunks of amber freshly mined. I see the blushing crimson leaves of the Persian ironwood that started their autumn tints as long ago as August. If I look from the window now, all I can see are stark, bare, black twigs. Oh for the summer.

Of favourite sights in pleasant places, there are plenty to recall: the simple pleasure of feathery cosmos with magenta flowers growing up through the seat of a white-painted wire-work garden bench; it was meant for two, but the cosmos took up one side of it, perforating the intricate curlicues of woven wire with their filigree foliage, topped by their smiling daisies of shocking pink. I smiled, too, whenever I sat next to them and looked them in their bright yellow eyes.

There was the joy of seeing a friend discover the rich, chocolate scent of their cousin, *Cosmos atrosanguineus*, and her sadness at finding that she could not get it through the winter, outdoors. A rooted cutting waits to surprise her in the spring.

Yes, the scents. The summer scents stay fresh in the memory. Clove pinks with their aromatic sweet confection of spicy perfume, or the light fragrance of sweet peas. Inhale deeply and try not to sniff in the black and glossy pollen beetle who has discovered the gourmet qualities of leguminous anthers.

There was a lavender that smelt just like eucalyptus; a eucalyptus that smelt just like lemons, and another plant, *Ozothamnus ledifolius*, that reeked of stewed prunes. Memories of my old school dinners, and custard with skin like a tough old piece of leather.

There were tobacco plants and old roses, some with perfume as subtle as a tin of cheap talcum powder. Unkind to grumble, I know, but some modern roses have an infinitely preferable apple scent. Autumn yielded the tumbling, honeyed leaves of *Cercidiphyllum japonicum*, the Katsura tree, whose falling foliage smells just like toffee apples; and before that, there were the apple-scented leaves of the rose 'Lady Penzance', much nearer to 'Cox's Orange Pippin' in fragrance than a crateful of bland 'Golden Delicious'.

The foreign apple may not be worth dreaming about, but foreign gardens certainly are. I can whisk myself back to the Caribbean where, in September, I trod the tropic turf. Hibiscus and ginger lilies pushed up their flamboyant flowers amid a thick, green, squeaky jungle of succulent foliage in the Flower Forest of Barbados. Lizards shot like darts across the trunks of the towering palm trees whose fat fans filtered the glare of the silver sun.

I can still inhale the sharp tang of nutmeg from Grenada, the Spice Island, and can still hear the empty shells the islanders used to cover their garden paths, crunching under my feet, as the log fire crackles.

The silky soft white sand can still be felt in between my toes, as can the slippery slimeyness of tropical mud after a down-pour. The feel of the saturated shirt that steamed when the sun came out again can still be brought to my daydreaming mind.

In South Africa, the rain rained and the wind blew as we battled in coaches around the Cape. But for one shining moment, it subsided as we climbed Table Mountain in the cable car and looked down from the grey and rocky summit at the blue of the bay below, through a lace doily of gossamer clouds.

There were orange sheets of daisies in Namaqualand, where the desert blooms once a year, and the sacred ibises strutted their stuff with the egrets on the lawns of Durban Botanic Gardens. Sunbirds and sugar birds flitted from flower to flower, sipping their fill of nectar.

Back home, the days grew shorter and the sparrows fluffed up their feathers as they sat on the bird table and demanded more seed. The leaves began to shudder and fall, having the grace to offer one last show before refusing to resume normal service until the spring.

And now they all sit quietly. Tree and shrub, bird and beast are silently dozing, remembering the pleasures that have gone before and that will, hopefully, come again. Until then, I must rely on those winter stalwarts: Suttons and Dobies, Unwins and Brown, Mr Fothergill's and Thompson & Morgan to keep the flame flickering as the fire dies and I doze off.

1997

A Tall Story

I've just bought my biggest tree ever. And I'm a bit ashamed. Well, you know, proper gardening is about growing things from seed or cuttings, or from young plants at the very least, and nurturing them, tending them and feeling justifiably rewarded when they thrive.

But then there are moments in one's life when patience, while not in short supply, is overruled. It occurs when patience will mean that something doesn't look right for the next ten years or more. Not until the plant in question has grown, put on weight and assumed a reasonable stature that's in scale with its surroundings. That's what goaded me into parting with ... No, I can't tell you how much it was, except that it ran into three figures.

I bought a bay tree. A bay tree that is 15 feet tall. "What?" I hear you exclaim. "A common-or-garden bay tree? The sort that can be rooted from cuttings with very little bother and a bit of bottom heat?"

Well, yes. And you can tell that I'm on the defensive here. You see, around the back of our barn we've just made a long sweep of gravel, where, at a pinch, visitors can park a car or two. And I wanted a focal point for it, one that would be tall enough to screen us from the windows of the house opposite. Oh, we get on all right, but I do like a bit of privacy, even from my closest friends.

It was Mrs T who, when I proposed a tree in a large tub, suggested an evergreen. It made sense. What's the point in having a focal point or a screen for only half the year when you could have it for the full 12 months provided you're prepared to do a bit of leaf sweeping in June? That's the thing about evergreens, they are considerate. They don't shed their old leaves when all the other trees are doing it. They realise you've got enough to do in autumn, so they obligingly wait until early summer before dumping their load.

Why a bay tree, rather than a holly or an evergreen oak? Well, because the plant centre had one in stock. And when I come to think about it, bay will fill out faster than holly, and won't drop quite as many leaves as an evergreen oak.

So there I was, mooching around the plant centre and perusing the price tags as closely as the plants. There was a wonderful cloud-pruned tree of *Ilex crenata*, a spineless small-leaved holly that looks a bit like classy privet. Six feet tall it was, just like something out of Noddy, and beautifully sculpted into random spheres that seemed to float in mid-air at the ends of its contorted branches. It wasn't quite tall enough, but oh, what a focal point. Then I saw the label. It was just £1 short of £3,000. I moved on.

There were tall lollipops of *Photinia x fraseri* 'Red Robin', but I've got a bit of a problem with that plant. It seems slightly tarty. A touch too much lipgloss to be respectable. What about a palm? *Trachycarpus fortunei* is tough enough, but I didn't want a Mediterranean feel behind my Hampshire barn. Then I saw it. The bay tree to end all bay trees, clipped into a 15-foot pyramid. I looked up at the towering canopy, then looked down at the price label, gulped, and reached for my chequebook.

It arrived the next day on a lorry. "Have you got a fork-lift truck?" I asked the driver. "No, mate. Just a pallet trolley." But the gravel path would ground any pallet trolley, so we rolled it, with much huffing and puffing, to the corner of the barn, some 50 yards from its ultimate destination.

That was yesterday. It's still there. I'm waiting for the arrival of half a dozen mates who can help me get the thing to its final resting place. Then I'll remove its pot and build a raised bed from railway sleepers. Rather a nifty wheeze I thought, rather than forking out for a container that would probably cost more than the tree.

I'm still not telling you how much. And I haven't told the wife yet, either. But should you see an advert in the back of this magazine asking for a home for a 15-foot bay tree, you'll know I've been rumbled. I'm rooting a few cuttings just in case.

[*cit*] 2005

What Lies Beneath

If there is one thing that no two gardeners seem to agree about it's flavour. Who can say whether anyone else's palate is in any way like one's own? What I regard as subtle, you may regard as insipid. What I consider to be tangy, you may well decide is just plain sour.

It set me thinking about what actually gives fruits and vegetables their flavour, and the answers I came up with may put you off your dinner.

You see, if you've ever grown tomatoes in greenhouse border soil that has been watered with a well-known proprietary disinfectant, you may well have noticed that the tomatoes themselves taste of disinfectant. It follows, therefore, that if you water your tomatoes with dilute sheep manure, then they are likely to taste of . . . well, you see what I mean.

All this business about organic growing is very interesting. If you swear by the flavour of organically grown crops, then what you are saying is that you prefer the flavour of blood, bone and fishmeal to that of Growmore. But is dried blood really more toothsome than sulphate of ammonia? Never having had a spoonful of either I'd be reluctant to say.

Some of the best grapes I ever tasted were from a vine that had been planted on top of a dead donkey, and an Irishman once told me that three dead dogs were essential under your 'Black Hamburgh' vine if it was to produce a good crop. It's reminiscent of that picture on the front of the Golden Syrup tin: "out of the strong came forth sweetness". Are those really flies buzzing around a dead lion?

My greatest treat this year was the first fig from a tree I planted against the house a few years ago. I plucked it on a warm summer's day and took it indoors to share with my mother-in-law. We both agreed that it was delicious, and then I recalled that I had planted it, on the advice of a friend, in a Gladstone bag sunk into the soil. Tender as my fig was, was I tasting nothing more than rotting leather?

When we used to walk along the riverbank in Yorkshire we would pass the filter beds where tomatoes grew in profusion, I remember remarking on the fact to my auntie. "Ooh yes," she said. "I hope nobody eats the fruits, after all, you know where the seeds have come from." I didn't at the time; but now I've had the time to work it out I can understand her distaste.

You know, I rather wish I'd not started down this road. Goodness knows how far the roots of an apple tree might spread, and what they might encounter on the way. You just can't be sure of anything these days.

[*cit*] 1994

Full House

Parkinson's Law suggests that, "work expands to fill the time available for its completion," which is a posh way of saying that if you have a lot of time you can do things more slowly.

Titchmarsh's Law is much more horticultural. Titchmarsh's Law says that however big your greenhouse you will always have too many plants to fit into it. To this end, last summer, I bought a new polythene tunnel so that, come April and May, by far the busiest months in my greenhouse, I would have enough room to allow for any expansion.

And what has happened? You've guessed. I have far too many plants to fit into my greenhouse and my new polythene tunnel. Never mind. One thing is certain though, and that is that both of them give me tremendous pleasure.

Each year when I journey down to the West Country on holiday, I marvel at all the tender plants that can be grown outdoors in those parts of Devon and Cornwall that enjoy the warming effects of the Gulf Stream. Oh how I yearn to grow palm trees and echiums outside all the year round, and enjoy the steadying effects on temperature that the sea bestows. But I can't. Instead I have greenhouses to shelter my tender plants and, on chilly winter days when snow is falling, winds are howling, or rain is being blown sideways across the garden, I open my greenhouse door and escape into another world.

I know that not everyone has discovered the pleasure of growing under glass, and this includes some folk who have a greenhouse. You can sometimes see these forlorn structures from the comfort of the train. They sit at the bottom of people's gardens, empty except for a few dirty seed trays and a plastic sprayer. There they stand, from October through until April, waiting for the annual crop of tomatoes. What a waste. I've never been as fond of tomatoes as I am of coleus and geraniums, fuchsias and begonias, mimosa and white jasmine.

I can hardly bring myself to bother with greenhouse tomatoes when I can enjoy these other beauties through the year without spending too much on heat.

In my Crystal Palace of a greenhouse at Barleywood I have three sections. One section is heated to a winter minimum of 7°C (45°F), one part to 10°C (50°F) and the central conservatory section hovers somewhere between the two. Tubular electric heaters are wired through a thermostat in the interests of saving money, and the whole system is run, at night, on Economy 7, the electricity board's most reasonably priced juice.

So, I enjoy the bright yellow flowers of mimosa and jasmine at the start of the year, and also manage to keep propagating a large collection of pelargoniums and fuchsias. This is courtesy of a heated propagator which ensures that when I need a bit more heat, it is provided, once more, as economically as possible.

Areas of slatted shelving underneath the staging allow tuberous begonias and freesias to dry off when their flowers fade, and I have two massive tanks, one at the end of each section, which collect rainwater. This can be pumped into my watering can with the aid of a bilge pump fastened to the staging. I enjoy this kind of self-sufficiency.

But it is not just the practicalities of a greenhouse that appeal; I like the silence. Open the door and walk inside and there is something almost holy about the whole atmosphere. Plants don't make noises like animals. They grow quietly. Half an hour in their company, pulling off faded leaves and flowers, sowing a few seeds or taking a few cuttings and I'm a new man.

Lots of gardeners like listening to the radio while they potter about. I never have. I like the thinking time that such quietude offers; my mind can wander over a topic for my next column, or plot for the next novel. I can think about my holidays, or think about nothing at all. I just slip into a sort of mindless limbo as I dibble around in the compost.

Maybe that's my problem. I like going into my greenhouse so much that I'm forever adding more plants, either as seedlings or as cuttings, and so the space quickly disappears. I've tried adding a few shelves at head height and filling up the cold frames outside the greenhouse with plants that can take lower temperatures. But it's no good. The spare patch of bench that I create one day is filled the next with something else. The same is true of my new tunnel.

It's fun really. I wonder if Sir Joseph Paxton had the same problem when he designed the original Crystal Palace?

1999

The Model Gardener

My body is something I have always tried to be fairly relaxed about. I'm not a fitness fanatic. There seems to me to be something faintly unhealthy about an obsessive interest in the curvature of one's bicep or trimness of one's torso and, anyway, as you get older, keeping it sculpted gets a lot harder. I try to convince myself that walking up and down my steep hillside of a garden, coupled with a moderate amount of spadework, will keep me in trim. I'm quite wrong, of course. It used to, but I have noticed, over the last few years, an extra inch or two creeping on to the waistline.

No matter. It is something I can hide with a generously proportioned sweatshirt and, when I have my photograph taken, I can expand my chest and allow the natural inflation of my upper torso to outdo my abdominal muscles, which is a roundabout way of saying that I've learnt to hold it in.

When I was a youth, working in a nursery, I weighed in at around eight stone for five years. I was only eight and a half stone when I got married. I am not eight and a half stone now, but I can afford a better wardrobe.

But just recently, an event occurred which meant that I could no longer hide behind my loose-fitting shirts. I was asked to pose for Madame Tussaud's, London. What a treat. What an honour. The last time I had been to their Baker Street premises, it was to attend the launch of Percy Thrower's autobiography, which I'd edited. Percy stood in a conservatory at Madame Tussaud's. The wax Percy, that is. He was the only gardener that they had ever included, and I was to be the second. Not bad, that.

I was invited to go along to be measured up and, on the appointed day, I duly made my way past the throng of tourists, mainly Japanese, outside Madame Tussaud's. It did occur to me that a goodly number of visitors would probably have no idea who I was. I mean, if they didn't recognise me in the flesh as I pushed past, how could they know me in wax? Ah well, perhaps gardeners go there, too, on occasion, and I might make them feel at home.

I was greeted warmly by the staff and taken through the gallery to be shown where I would be positioned. With relief we walked past the Chamber of Horrors – well, you can't be too sure – and into a gallery where tourists milled around the likenesses of Pierce Brosnan, Joanna Lumley and Brad Pitt.

"This is where you'll be," I was informed. I warmed to them. They clearly knew my real station in life. "We're going to turn this area into a garden party, and we want you to be a part of it."

"What, with Brad Pitt and Pierce Brosnan?"

"Yes."

Percy never had it so good. Then came the downside to all this.

"We would like to build a replica of your shed and have you posing by it while the others are out in the garden." Only fair I suppose. Putting me in my place.

I was taken to be photographed on a balcony. Then we came back indoors.

"We thought you might like to pose like this," said a girl with a photo of me leaning on a hoe.

"Fine."

"So could you lean on this one while we measure you?" She offered a hoe and I leaned on it, standing on a turntable which was rotated a little at a time while I was photographed and videoed from every angle, and my face was measured with callipers. It was like being judged at Crufts.

The photographer snapped away. Thorough these folk were, then I realised just how thorough.

"Look, I'm sorry to have to ask you this," said the sculptor who was to create my portrayal, Louis Wiltshire, "but we like to get the body absolutely right, so would you mind posing in a pair of shorts?"

Of course, it could have been a wind-up. Whatever it was, I reluctantly and rather bashfully agreed, which is why, on a sunny summer's day, I found myself standing on a turntable, leaning on a hoe, wearing nothing more than a pair of Lycra shorts and a nervous smile.

"It makes the clothes hang more authentically if we get the body right," they reassured me.

The indignity over, I was pounced on by ladies who checked the colour of my hair. "You don't dye it?" "No." They also checked my skin tones and my eyes.

Then they let me put my clothes on again and asked me to sign the visitor's book. I flipped through the previous pages that included Tim Henman, Prince Andrew and Sophie Rhys-Jones and wondered if they had worn the same shorts.

I was asked if I would come back for a second sitting. Oh, and could I supply them with some clothes? I happily agreed and I'm now getting picky about my wardrobe and very aware of the shape of my body.

So, should you find yourself in the middle of a garden party at Madame Tussaud's, and spot me near Pierce and

Brad, just remember that what you see is accurate, and that if you put your arm around my waist, you'll know the truth of it.

[*cit*] 2001

Living with the Enemy

Sticking up for wildlife is all very well, but sometimes they have plenty of other people sticking up for them too. Take bats. Did you know that if you have bats in your house or in an outbuilding on your land they are protected? And that you can be fined or sent to prison if you do anything to harm them? Well, it's true. It's certainly a salutary thought.

There I was, ready to convert this old barn at our new house. I thought we'd better have someone from English Nature round to check it out, and only then did it all become clear. I thought we were just being considerate. It didn't occur to me that we had legal obligations.

The roof of the barn needs to be removed, strengthened and replaced. The council has given its permission. But the presence of the bats means we must do the job between the beginning of March and the end of May when they are most likely to be out and about.

But try telling that to a builder. Well, he'll have to get his act together because that's what the law says and, for once, I'm rather pleased with the law.

I say bats, although the reality of the situation is that we are talking in the singular here. They come and go apparently, and at the moment there is only one in evidence. Well, its droppings anyway. I watched as the conservationist's eyes lit up when he showed me the little black sausage in his hand. If you've ever seen a mouse dropping you will know what a bat dropping looks like. Except that when you rub a bat's dropping between your fingers it turns to dust and reveals the little wings and bits and pieces of the thousands of midges that a bat can eat in a single night. I reckon it must go along with its mouth wide open, like some monstrous whale devouring krill.

Towards the end of summer I stood outside the house, opposite the yew trees, and watched a couple of bats doing their aerobatics. They must have nipped over from the church across the road. Prospecting probably.

I hope they can wait for the builders to leave before they decide to take up residence, unless they are already in the house itself, although the pest-control man assured me that there was no sign of them there.

You see, that's another quandary. Keen naturalist that I am, I was unwilling to give the woodworm and death-watch beetle any quarter. They've eaten at least half the beams away already, and I'm rather keen to hang on to the rest for my own pleasure and for the safety of my nearest and dearest. I may be a devout organic gardener, but when it comes to my beams, chemicals win every time.

Now that all of the creepy-crawlies have been bumped on the head and the nice man in the overalls has handed me the guarantee, I am a confirmed organic gardener again. But then gardeners often have to make choices that are a touch unfair on the wildlife. We love butterflies, but are less concerned about moths. Why? I suspect it's because they have duller livery and fly at night, seemingly unwilling to share their lives with us.

We love the blackbird when he perches on the chimney top and sings his twilight song, and we curse him when he eats our raspberries. We love the mole in *Wind in the Willows* but hate him when he digs up the lawn.

Living with animals, birds and insects is something we all have to do. The trouble is that today we are encouraged to believe that we do not need to compromise. We have so much control over some of the major elements in our lives that we think it unfair when our needs are sacrificed at the altar of nature.

A few weeks ago, my daughter was due to visit friends in the West Country. The weather turned foul. "But I have to go," she insisted. "I told them I would and I can't let them down." It was a few minutes before I could convince her that, in spite of our modern technology and supreme intellectual power over other beings, there are times when nature flexes her muscles and it's best to give in.

She was shocked at first, and probably a little irritated. She has grown up in an age when we can generally go where we please, when we please. She watched as the weather got worse, and by evening she admitted the decision to stay at home was a wise one.

It does us good now and again to realise that there are greater forces than our own at work. The weather that day was a case in point. And so are the bats. I'll be happy to share my roof with them, provided they make sure that their holidays last the full two months.

That's a thought. If they come back early and my builder hasn't finished, do I stand a chance of being sent down? Maybe I'll ring my travel agent. Does my holiday insurance cover the bats that live with me?

2003

MARCH

The Long Game

Lack of confidence is a funny thing, and manifests itself in different ways. Some folk become shrinking violets and others appear robust and opinionated, but both traits can be no more than a means of self-defence, masking an insecurity that leaves them feeling vulnerable and inadequate.

Now don't imagine that I have started writing an agony column. No. It's just that I've had a friend round to look at the garden and was suddenly made aware of the fact that, as yet, I'm a bit defensive about it.

It's now two years since we moved here. In that time we've had to completely renovate the house, and the barn where I now write, and the garden has been developed at the same time. The house is roughly in the centre of the plot, so it has garden on all sides. A pleasant change from our last place where the garden rose up a steep hill at the rear.

I've not rushed at it like a bull at a gate. It seemed foolish to dig out beds and borders before I was certain of the pattern of the sun during the day, and the exact features I wanted to include. But then I've not been idle, either. We have an octagonal pale blue summerhouse, a fully functional and pretty handsome greenhouse, a circular pool with a fountain, a bed of tree ferns underneath the old yew tree, and assorted beds and borders sculpted where I think they will work best. There's a terrace, studded with topiary box bushes in orbs and pyramids. But the overall plan is not yet complete, and the structure is not totally in place.

You'll understand my reluctance, then, to show folk around. But my friend was insistent. He came for lunch, with his wife. He's a good mate of long-standing, 20 years or more, and he's a garden designer.

He was champing at the bit to get out there the moment he arrived, but lunch was almost ready, and so he contained himself until it was over, then stood up and said, "Right! Can I see the garden now?"

Reluctantly I rose to my feet and went out with him. I felt rather like an estate agent, pointing out the many possibilities of a plot that is, as yet, relatively undeveloped. And yet, in spite of my boyish enthusiasm, there was upon his face a look of disappointment he found hard to mask. At least I think there was. Maybe I am being oversensitive.

You see, our last garden took 20-odd years to get right. Well, yes, it looked good after five years, but by the time we left it had seen two decades of growth. My new garden isn't likely to mirror its predecessor's maturity in a couple of seasons.

But then my friend would have known that. Why, then, do I think it fell short of his expectations? Well, because I had not divided it up into little rooms. Along with him I've been exhorting folk to fill their garden full of secret corners and surprises for years, and sometimes this can be achieved by dividing them up into compartments. But not always.

Just because Vita Sackville-West did it at Sissinghurst, and Lawrence Johnston did it at Hidcote does not mean I have to do it. I don't want a series of green-walled cupboards that interrupt the view. I want long views and vistas, rather than cosy corners.

I wonder if it has something to do with being brought up in houses with tiny gardens. Now, all I want is space and light, and when I have it, it seems perverse to cut it out. My friend, on the other hand, was born in a large house set in stately acres. Maybe that's why he wants a garden of tiny rooms. Perhaps the whole thing is to do with fighting against your parents. Hang on. Perhaps this *is* an agony column.

It would not be so bad if he was the only visitor who, as yet, could not quite see the potential of my plot. Three ladies came to call last May. Again they were revered professionals who had come to have a dekko. I walked them around the garden that had been barely a year in the making. They wrote us a lovely thank you letter, praising Mrs T's home-made Florentines. They didn't mention the garden.

And so, when next you are embarrassed by the state of your embryonic plot when visitors come around, rest assured you are not on your own. Hang on to that fragile vestige of confidence and don't forget nature is there to offer a helping hand. She alone will understand your long-term plans and help them come to fruition.

In the meantime, do as I am doing and decline any requests to "see how it is coming along." Don't let 'em in until you've done it. Of course I won't be able to stick to it. But I am looking forward to the first person saying, "Wow! What a wonderful garden." It can't be too far off.

2005

It's a Man Thing

The collecting bug. I think it's a man thing. Women are much less acquisitive. Except, perhaps, when it comes to shoes. And handbags. But men can collect anything. And I mean, anything.

I think it must be a primitive urge, some sort of primal instinct. The more that you hoard around yourself, the more chance you stand of being able to protect your tribe from any eventuality. Yes, 152 varieties of pelargonium is sure to make me a better father. Mmm.

But there must be a reason for it somewhere, rather than simply an honest passion for one particular kind of plant. I mean, I do love pelargoniums, partly because I have a sentimental attachment to them since they are one of the first plants I ever grew, partly because they are easy to cultivate, and partly because they are such beautiful plants.

But do I really need 152 of them? Clearly I do, because ever since I put the order in last week I have been feeling this warm kind of glow. I've been anticipating the moment when they will arrive, and I shall be potting them up. I shall put them in clay pots, in compost that I have mixed myself, and I shall label them uniformly with white tags and thick indelible pen.

Then I shall arrange them on the greenhouse staging at a perfectly symmetrical spacing, and pot them on as they grow until I have a house full of flowering pelargoniums. Sad? Not a bit of it. Primal? Maybe, but I'm unrepentant about my passion.

The thing is, I would not feel the same about the plants if all 152 were the same variety. That would just be a lot of plants. Not a collection. It is the comprehensiveness of the selection that gives me the thrill, and that is the difference between someone who grows plants and someone who collects them.

I class myself as nothing more than a gardener, but I suppose the pelargoniums are a bit of a lapse. I don't have this urge to collect every kind of snowdrop or ancient apple variety, probably because in the first instance I can't tell them apart, and in the second I have no room for a large orchard. But I can sympathise with the people who do. Up to a point.

I mean, I heard the other day of a nursery in Oregon that grows 500 or more different heucheras. Heucheras! I ask you. When you've seen one you've seen them both. It's the same with sempervivums and hostas. Oh, don't get me wrong, I love both of them, but not in their hundreds. The Japanese and the Americans are crazy about hostas and keep on raising them. One little variation in leaf size or variegation is enough to make a new variety, but you'd probably need a magnifying glass, not to mention a rainy afternoon, to tell them apart.

At least a collection of pot-grown plants means that your garden can still look like a garden, with decent swathes of things. Start collecting garden plants and the outlook will become something akin to a Seurat painting: spotty.

"This garden boasts 500 varieties of rose" is a phrase that makes my heart sink. You know the chances are that they have been plonked in with little thought to their health or overall effect, and that the most important thing is that every one will have a properly engraved label. The prospect of 500 twiggy bushes with little in between does not constitute a proper plant collection. Care and standard of cultivation is important to a real collector, and so is the way in which the collection enhances the garden.

Some blokes collect grasses, others are deeply into alpines. Those who collect dwarf conifers are now in the minority, or in a mental home. Large conifers I can understand, they are majestic giants of the landscape, but collecting dwarf conifers is only one step up from collecting garden gnomes, and we all know what the Royal Horticultural Society thinks of them. Me? I have two gnomes, and that in no way constitutes a collection. They sit under shrubs, ready to bring a smile to the lips of anyone who thinks my garden is too classy to give them a home.

I suppose some women do collect plants, but they are in the minority. It's blokes who salivate at the prospect of a stamp or coin collection. It is men who cultivate hundreds of different dahlias or chrysanthemums, and women who cultivate sighs.

They will never understand the macho need to have a lot of anything, but then that is just as well. The prospect of a household where the man presides over a thousand varieties of daffodil and the woman, tulips, promises to leave both fighting for every inch of border soil. It wouldn't work if women were into collection, too. Vive la difference I say. And vive la pelargonium!

2004

A Passion for Alpines

This is usually the time of year when I start pining for the mountains. It must be something to do with the fact that I was born on the edge of Ilkley Moor; not exactly in the heather, but in a maternity home that was surrounded by the stuff. When you are born at a relatively high altitude it's hardly surprising that you should develop a fondness for alpine plants and each spring my passion for them rises.

I've been a member of the Alpine Garden Society for more than twenty years and I once managed to grow and exhibit a few choice alpines at one of its shows. I didn't come away with any prizes, but it gave me far more of a buzz than I would have achieved had I been growing chrysanthemums.

You see, when it comes to growing for showing, pot-grown alpines are the Fabergé eggs of the gardening world. I can't tell you the pleasure it gives me to get my nose right down to their level and scrutinise a potful of some intricate mound-forming treasure that is studded with tiny flowers. If the plant is tricky to grow, and many of them are, so much the better; the sense of achievement is heightened.

It is further enhanced by the fact that many need protection from wet weather in the form of a cold frame or alpine house. The gems of the plant world are best displayed to the world in glass-topped jewel cases.

Now you might regard this as an additional expense, and indeed it is, but it is also a way of adding to the pleasure. I can think of nothing more satisfying on a crisp, spring day, than walking into a small wooden greenhouse with grit-filled benches down each side holding flower-pots bristling with high mountain beauties.

In such a situation alpine plants are presented to you in all their perfection and you can rub your hands together and gloat as the buds on your androsaces and dionysias, drabas and lewisias burst into bloom.

But the first pleasure is choosing the plants from an alpine nursery catalogue. You can savour each description as though it were a recipe for an exotic dish. Then there's the thrill when your alpines arrive through the post. Don't be shocked, you can pick them up from an alpine nursery, if there is one nearby, but a number of alpine growers have been supplying plants by mail-order for half a century and they are past masters at packing them so that they arrive, not only swiftly, but in perfect condition to grow on.

Alpine growers, more than any other kind of gardener, have their secrets of success. Their composts are hand-mixed and comprise everything from crushed charcoal and brick dust to oyster shell and leaf-mould, depending on the precise predilections of the plants being grown.

Plastic pots are seldom used. You wouldn't wrap a Fabergé egg in polythene, would you? No, it is terracotta for these precious plants, generously crocked in the bottom of the pot and finished off at the top with sharp grit to prevent them from being splashed by mud and to show off the neat rosettes of leaves.

Alpine growing is undoubtedly a sport for the perfectionist. There are so many areas where excellence can be achieved. It is not just in the growing of the plants, but in the preparation of the compost, the cleanliness of the pots, the uniformity of the gritty top-dressing and even in the writing of the plant labels.

You see, label writing is an art form in itself. Do you choose plastic or anodised aluminium? Oh, aluminium I think. Do you write on them in indelible felt tip, soft pencil or Indian ink? The last two for preference. Unless, of course, you are one of those lucky junk shop hunters who has managed to come across an old-fashioned labelling machine which stamps the plant names on strips of lead. Now that's real class.

But the thing which will single you out from all other gardens is your skill in growing the really tricky alpines. Some of them are far from keen on being grown away from their mountain habitats, so it is especially rewarding if you can cultivate a perfect hemisphere of *Dionysia aretioides*, which in spring is covered in bright yellow flowers.

It is not, I freely admit, something which I have yet achieved but I know a few folk who have and each spring my eyes turn in their direction, or rather in the direction of their plants. I am not a man given to envy as a rule, but the sight of such a plant, well grown and in full flower, can make my fingers itch uncontrollably. Perhaps if I'd been born in a maternity home surrounded by allotments I'd have felt the same about rhubarb.

1996

Grown with Laughter

Can plants make you laugh? Not quite, but some can make you smile. I feel in need of them whenever I've been over-long in the company of po-faced gardeners who tend to take themselves too seriously and wax lyrical about things green and brown. This doesn't happen very often, but I'm still happy to grow any plant that gives me a bit of a giggle.

The first one I encountered as an innocent youth was *Dicentra spectabilis*, the bleeding heart. At first glance the pendent, locket-shaped flowers seem to live up to their common name, but if a single flower is removed and held upside down the impression is different.

When I was first shown this trick I could see what I took to be a lady in a rather bouffant wig sitting in a Barbara Cartland-pink bath. But then I was told that it was not the lady's head I could see, but her pale arms clasping a sponge above her body which was hidden from view. Naughty but nice, that's dicentra. I still keep peeping down into the bath, but the definition of her body remains hazy.

Some plants can make you smile because of their scent. I'm not thinking of the pure pleasure of border pinks or freesias, but of unexpected pongs like those you'll get from *Ozothamnus ledifolius*. This is the plant whose fading flowers smell of stewed prunes. I hated them at school. This plant doesn't so much make me smile as grimace.

I much prefer the aroma of camomile, which smells just like those sweets we used to have called Spangles, or heliotrope which is redolent of Play-Doh. Then there is the Katsura tree, *Cercidiphyllium japonicum*, whose fallen leaves smell like toffee apples. Less romantic people describe it as burnt sugar, but it's toffee apples and fairgrounds to me.

Touch-me-not, impatiens, can make children and some unsuspecting grown-ups laugh when it expels its seeds from fat pods, snapping them open and hurling out its bounty like bullets. The touch-me-not has given a cheap thrill to many a maiden aunt.

Squirting cucumbers are better, though less frequently grown. When the stalk of the ripe fruit of *Ecballium elaterium* is snapped off, its seeds are squirted out with all the energy of a clown squirting water from his mouth.

It would be much kinder, perhaps, to settle for *Mimosa pudica*, the sensitive plant, which has finely fingered leaves that gently fold up when they are touched. Easy to locate in the seed catalogues and easy to grow, this plant has enthused many a small child with the pleasures of gardening and it is hardly rude enough to offend the most sensitive relation.

Aside from the misshapen carrots and potatoes so beloved of Esther Rantzen on *That's Life*, I can think of no other plants that are saucy, except, of course, anthuriums. I got myself into regal hot water with these. You know what it's like. Suddenly you find your tongue leading you down a path that would do better unexplored. Something tells you it will all end in tears and it usually does. In my case I like to think I got away with it.

I'd just been presented to HRH the Queen Mother at a charity reception. We were standing in front of a bank of the aforesaid blooms and the Queen Mother said to me "Lovely flowers." Instead of simply saying, "Yes, aren't they," I found myself telling Her Majesty the story of CH Cook and Queen Mary.

CH Cook was Percy Thrower's future father-in-law and head gardener at Windsor Castle back in the 1920s and 30s. Queen Mary, accompanied by the King, was being taken on a tour of the greenhouses one day and encountered a vast display of anthuriums of which the gardeners, one of them being Percy Thrower, were very proud.

Queen Mary clearly did not share their sentiments. "Cook!" she commanded. "Have these taken away, terribly rude-looking things!"

It's a nice story, but perhaps not one you should tell to the Queen Mother. She smiled at me sweetly and passed on to a man standing by some chrysanthemums. Anthuriums still make me break out in a cold sweat to this day.

1997

Nature or Nurture?

The Americans talk about green thumbs. In Britain, we talk about green fingers. But whichever digits are verdant, is it really true? Is there such a thing as a green-fingered gardener, or does it all boil down to knowledge and acquired skill?

I have no doubts about it at all; I think some people are born green-fingered and others, however hard they try to acquire them, will never be in the same league.

Any good gardener with keen powers of observation will have noticed, during the course of his or her life, that there are some people who seem to be naturally at home with plants and others who just do not look comfortable among them. I am not talking here about people who admit that they are indifferent to plants and gardens, far from it. I have watched people who are keen and even knowledgeable growers wander among their charges looking somehow out of place.

A lot of it is down to body language. The formative years of my gardening training were conducted in a potting shed. Don't panic, there are no sordid stories coming up. Here, I worked alongside two or three gardeners who had a real feeling for plants. Watch them knock a pelargonium out of a pot, or hack it to bits for cuttings and you could see a sort of slap-dash but confident abandon about their workmanship. The nearest thing I can compare this with is the mother of a large family.

While the parents of just one or two children will tend to fuss and cluck over their progeny, the mothers and fathers of large families must somehow divide their time up into even smaller fragments. And yet the children of such large broods, so often scooped up in careless armloads when they are small and fed in something resembling a works canteen, grow into self-assured beings because of the relaxed confidence with which they were brought up.

Alright, so it's a generalisation, but you know what I mean. Ma Larkin was probably a great gardener.

At the other end of the scale, I have watched trainee gardeners being taught how to take a cutting or sow seeds. They copy keenly what they think they have been shown, and yet it looks all wrong. It's rather like watching a ballet dancer who has a brilliant technique, but no soul.

Potting is the one task which, I think, separates the greenfingered from the brown. It is all down to the handling of the pot and the way the compost is fed in and firmed around the roots of the plant. The classic giveaway to a brown-fingered gardener is the patting down of the compost on the surface, and the use of the flat ends of the fingers rather than the vertical use of the fingertips.

Watching a good gardener at the potting bench is as pleasurable as watching a good chef conjure up a meal over the stove.

I don't want to sound elitist and snobbish about this, and I assure you that it is no affectation. Nothing gives me greater pleasure than to see a gardener who is green-fingered. "But just a minute," I hear you say. "You're not talking about green fingers here, you are talking about a basic gardening technique." Well, yes, I am in part, but the way in which an operation is carried out is often a good indicator of the colour of the fingers.

Most people, whatever shade their digits, can usually manage to sow a seed or plant a plant. Green fingers proper go much further than this. Take plants that are generally accepted as difficult to grow. Some gardeners, with great minds and plenty of horticultural knowledge, can tell you exactly what you should do to achieve your goal, and yet they cannot achieve it themselves. Others, who may not know the ins and outs of the plant quite so well, somehow have a feeling for it and manage to get it to grow. It is not something they have been taught, it is an inbuilt aptitude. Thanks to this, such gardeners can root the most difficult cuttings, or germinate the most resolutely slumbering seeds. Irritating isn't it? But it's true.

But there is one thing that baffles me. The one group of gardeners who seem to have the greenest fingers of all are the little old ladies. Now why should that be? Answers on a post-card, please.

1998

Getting a Hedge in Gardening

Being a hedge must be a bit like being an MP. I mean, let's face it, few of them are glamorous and at least one of them has had a very bad press. But then, to be fair, lots of them get on very quietly doing a good job for the people who put them in, and it's high time they were given a little praise. I am talking about hedges here.

Now let's tackle the controversial one first: Leyland cypress, the Rottweiler of the garden. Poor thing. It does exactly what is asked of it. It grows quickly and densely and makes a perfect screen. The trouble is that many owners don't realise that it is like the fairytale magic porridge pot that could not stop producing porridge. The Leyland cypress just won't stop growing, or at least not until it gets to 30m (100ft) or more. Mmmm. Tricky, unless you have the sense to cut it off in its prime at about 2m (6½ft) and then keep on top of it, literally. If you do that it makes the densest green barrier you've ever seen. Legislate against the Leyland cypress? No way. It's the owners we should be legislating against.

But as Leyland hedges are being ripped out all over the country, what is replacing them? Interwoven fencing. Shame. Instead of living in a woodland clearing, garden owners who replace their hedges with fences are living inside wooden boxes. What's more, all the environmental advantages of a hedge are lost. Very little lives on a fence. It can support a few overwintering ladybirds and earwigs in its crevices, but the only thing that can live inside it are wood-boring beetles, and even they don't much like the taste of tanalised timber. A light garnish of creosote isn't your average grub's idea of tomato sauce.

So let's do our bit to put the hedge back into the British landscape. Farmers have been ripping them up for years. It's not their fault, modern agriculture has demanded it. But wise farmers, the real custodians of the land, make provision to hang on to hedges wherever possible. Hedges are nature's motorways, allowing the flow of insect, bird and mammal traffic across the countryside.

Gardeners can do their bit, too, by replacing old and worn-out fences with hedges. Yes, I realise that in small gardens hedges can be difficult to accommodate. If your borders are narrow, the roots of the hedge can rob them of nutrients and suck them dry of moisture. But you can make provision to ensure this doesn't happen. First, dig the trench in which you're going to plant your hedge, and enrich it with well-rotted compost or manure to give the plants a good start in life. Next, slide a row of slates, corrugated iron or some other impenetrable barrier into the garden side of the trench to prevent the encroachment of roots into the border. If you do this, then the hedge should become a sympathetic backdrop to the border without stealing all its sustenance.

If you live in the country, try to plant a mixed native hedge, such as hawthorn, which will produce berries for the birds, and blackthorn, which will produce sloes for your gin. Holly will keep out next door's pets and provide food and shelter for the birds, as well as a glossy winter countenance. Add to these the spindle bush for its spectacular autumn tints and luminous winter fruits, the wayfaring tree, *Viburnum lantana*, and the field maple for even greater variety, and suddenly you have a much more interesting garden boundary than dreary old privet.

Oh, I know privet always looks smart, if it's well clipped, and it keeps most of its leaves in winter, but it's not exactly exciting, either from our point of view or that of the birds. A mixed native hedge will keep them much happier and, as a result, will keep you more enthralled with their activity.

Hedges like this don't need to be crisply clipped twice a year. You can give them one rough trim over in winter to keep them within bounds, and they'll be used by birds and butterflies, hedgehogs and beetles, field mice and other little residents of the countryside, even in the heart of a large town.

Take a look at your garden. Can you fit in a mixed hedge somewhere and do your bit for wildlife? You can even order your plants in advance to get cracking with the planting come the autumn.

Just like frogs, who seem to know when a garden pond has been installed, so other forms of wildlife will soon cotton on to the fact that you've provided them with a haven. And if you've never tasted sloe gin, you've never lived.

2000

The Cupboard Under the Stairs

Money isn't everything; it can't buy enthusiasm. I mused on this fact recently as I sipped yet another glass of Australian Chardonnay and realised how predictable I had become as an oenophile. I'll splash out every now and again: a warm, thick Shiraz in winter, a glass of Rioja in summer, a light-hearted bottle or two of Beaujolais, I even enjoy fresh-faced Pouilly-Fumé and Pouilly-Fuissé with fish. But I'm nothing like as adventurous as I used to be.

That was when we had no money at all and I had to make my own wine. There's nothing quite like a shortage of funds to make a gardener innovative when it comes to concocting a libation from a trugful of produce.

I was reminded of this over the weekend when I read about a competition for home-made wines in one of the Sunday newspapers. Here were delicious confections of pear and orange, blackberry and elderberry, crab apple and pomegranate.

It took me back to the early days of my marriage and the cupboard under the stairs. That's when my wine-making was at its zenith. There, among the floor mops and feather dusters, I would line up my demi-johns. Until I began making wine I thought demi-johns were an item of winter underwear. Among the cleaning impedimenta, my fat-bellied jars with their convoluted air locks would burble and bubble promisingly for weeks. When the bubbling stopped, I knew the contents were ripe for bottling.

To start with, I was quite circumspect. The basis of Château Beech Hill Road was a can of Boots' concentrate, some sugar, water and other bits and bobs. There was something called finings which made cloudy wine clear, and you could buy special corking outfits.

The inspiration for home wine-making came from my landlady at Kew. Not for her the tin can from the chemist, nor the wine lock from the research laboratory. Her demi-johns were fuelled by oak leaves and their necks sealed with a plug of cotton wool. She made her wines in rather a slapdash way, seemingly paying no heed to the importance of sterility, whereas for the duration of my wine-making I all but lived inside an autoclave.

I can remember sitting down with her on the veranda of her tiny terraced house which overlooked the tennis courts, and sipping the oak leaf wine when it had reached maturity. Innocuous it looked. Almost as clear as water, with a wonderfully sweet fragrance that gently nipped at the upper nasal passages.

Two glasses later I realised that it was, indeed, possible for eight people to play tennis with two balls and that I would have to learn to walk all over again. The journey down from the first-floor veranda was accomplished only after much eyeball screwing. The steps seemed to have doubled in number during our imbibing and were no longer placed at an equidistant spacing.

My landlady made wine from almost everything in her garden, from rose petals to lettuces. It was impossible not to be inspired, so one day I had a go myself with the grapes from a 'Brandt' vine outside my in-laws' house. It was a good summer, 1976, and the vine had cropped better than ever. My father-in-law was at a loss as to what to do with the bounty.

"I'll make wine," I rashly offered. And so the grapes were plucked from their rods and ferried home in two buckets to be offered in sacrifice at the feet of the god Bacchus. I trampled them in their buckets, but you'll be relieved to hear I used my bare hands rather than my feet. Then I carefully strained the juice into a couple of demi-johns and added water. Did I add anything else? I can't remember. I do remember deciding that I would add no fancy bits, believing that the grape skins would have imparted all that was necessary during the crushing process.

Fermentation was short. As I recall, the bubbling stopped within the week and I transferred the clear, sparkling contents to bottles. I read somewhere that my wine would probably be better drunk young, so after a respectable few weeks I took around some bottles for my father-in-law to sample.

Although he was not a wine connoisseur, he was certainly partial to the odd drop. A friend of his who was there at the time was also offered a glass. We all sipped. The friend looked a little quizzical and then sipped again.

"What's the story behind this?" he asked. I proudly explained that I had made it myself from a local crop of grapes.

"Where did they come from?"

I pointed at the vine on the other side of the window. He looked again at the wine in his glass and took another sip. "Hmmm," he said. "Doesn't travel well, does it?"

1999

APRIL

I'll Do It My Way

The archetypal image of a gardener is of a calm and placid sort of being; one who has infinite patience, boundless good humour and who is generally at ease with the world. But as anyone who has ever picked up a spade knows, there are moments when a calm frame of mind deserts us, and where tempers fray to the point of unravelling.

The reason for this temporary lapse in equilibrium can be attributed to all manner of causes. Slug and snail attack can reduce the sunniest soul to a gibbering wreck; vine weevil can do the same. But from time to time the spur is simply the activities of another gardener.

Gardeners, you see, are as territorial as any robin. Within their own patch they can be as happy as Larry, but let any interloper interfere with their cultivations and they turn from easy-going son or daughter of the soil into a malevolent force for retribution. Even if the perceived competition comes from someone they employ, they are likely to find it hard to curb their discontent.

The trouble is no two gardeners do the same job in the same way. Take mowing. Which way do you like your stripes? Or which bit of grass do you cut first, and which last? For men, this is like shaving. I always start underneath my left ear. Nothing in the world would induce me to start under my right. Similarly, in the garden the patch of lawn outside the back door is where I begin the mowing operation, finishing off by going round and round the circular pool with its cherub fountain until I disappear into the shed.

I could no more start with the cherub and end with the back door than I could fly to the moon. Daft? Yes. Unreasonable? You bet, but if it's all the same to you that's the way it should be done. If my man Bill ever mows the lawn because I have a deadline to catch and I'm stuck in the barn writing, I'd rather not look. He might cut it the wrong way round.

It was just the same when Chris Beardshaw, Joe Swift and Rachel de Thame used to come to Barleywood to film *Gardeners' World*. Now, they are all good gardeners and know one end of a spade from another, but they don't do things the same way as I do.

I mean, if you watch Chris bash the living daylights out of the rootball of a tree before he plants it, you could be forgiven for assuming that he was a karate champion in a former life.

Me? I come from the school that planted bare-root stock and nothing else until the late 1960s when container-grown plants took off. We treated such rootballs with respect in those days, disturbing them as little as possible. Today we've learned that in order to encourage the roots to explore from the hole, they need to be teased out of the rootball a little. Teased? Beardshaw torments them.

Then there are Rachel's gloves. She won't touch the soil without them. Me? I can't feel things property when I'm wearing gloves so I get stuck in bare-handed. Then I chomp into an apple. Result? I get tetanus and Rachel stays healthy, but at least I get to feel what I'm doing.

You see, when you analyse it like this it's unreasonable isn't it? Other gardeners, while operating differently, can do things just as effectively. It's just we don't like to admit it. We get set in our ways.

At least I'm aware that I have quirks, although whether it's wise to confess them to you I'm not sure. But then if everybody else has them, too, perhaps you'll look upon me with a benevolent smile.

Among the things that rattle me most are concerned with soil preparation. For a start, I can't stand footprints left over newly forked soil, or soil that is forked over unevenly, with lots of hillocks and hollows. I do not like to see soil raked, except when sowing seeds, or mulch that is applied unevenly.

I do not like to see fish ponds covered with netting, however predatory the local heron has become. What is the point in having a beautiful pond if its appearance is totally marred by plastic netting? Let the heron eat all the fish and enjoy a plain sheet of water, for goodness' sake.

Then there is staking. A good plant support is like a good wig; if you don't notice it, then it is doing its job properly. But some folk will find a great lump of wood and a bit of orange string to tie up a plant that looks like toppling. Result? Something akin to a turkey roast, trussed up this way and that, and anything but natural. The plant would look far better lying on the ground.

You could be forgiven for assuming, from this little tirade, that I am a hard man to please. But you'd be wrong. I am as reasonable as the next gardener, provided things are done the way I like them. Funny how other people don't always see it that way.

2005

Opening Up

I've just been asked to go public. In the nicest possible way. Would I open up my garden for a local charity? Now, before I rush headlong into this commitment with a feeling of euphoria brought on by someone thinking my garden is worth visiting, it will be as well for me to consider just what this will mean.

I have friends who open up their gardens, and the stories they can tell would curl the hair of a gooseberry. They'll remember a day when three old ladies were found, not locked in the lavatory, but wandering around the bedrooms long after all other guests had gone home for tea.

They'll advise you to draw your curtains, not only to deter local felons intent on a recce, but also to prevent the well-intentioned from making disparaging remarks about the colour of your emulsion in relation to the choice of upholstery fabric.

Old hands will advise the stockpiling of Harpic and Brobat should you be prepared to offer the facilities of the smallest room in the house, and they will recommend a smile and a polite refusal to guests who ask for a reduction on leaving because the roses weren't quite out.

All this is new to me. I have had a group or two around my garden – the local Horticultural Society of which I am an *in absentia* president (it seemed the least I could do), and a group of Hardy Plant Society aficionados (they have to be hardy to climb my hill). But that's not the same as nailing posters to telegraph poles, alerting the local papers and wantonly advertising the fact that you are open to inspection by supporters of the St John's Ambulance Brigade.

Take the admission fee. Is £1 too much? Surely not. It is for charity after all. Ah, but the local manor house is only charging 75p and they have four acres and a ruined chapel, too.

Do we provide teas? My wife's horror-stricken face suggested that we did not, but that the paddock could be used for picnics. Is our garden suitable for wheelchairs? Most definitely not (unless they are turbo-powered or pushed by someone called Arnold Schwarzenegger).

And then there's the question of plants. Do we sell them? "Considering you've spent the last ten years buying them, I think probably not." My wife has not yet discovered the joys of propagating plants.

I'm still in the throes of thinking about it, but one thing is for sure. I have developed a high regard for all those folk who, year after year, allow their gardens to be published in the yellow book.

All 2,500 gardens are open in aid of District Nurses. And if I open mine I shall probably be in need of one.

1991

Tree People

Experience is a funny thing. There is nothing more enrich-ing. If you make a botch of something, you learn from your mistake, and if you do something that works you know from experience that you have a tried-and-tested technique on your hands. You have acquired a skill. That's the theory anyway, and nowhere is experience more valuable than in the craft of gardening. Usually.

You see, there are pitfalls for the unwary. Once you start believing that your experience counts for everything, you are on a hiding to nothing. Why do I say this? On account of a bit of tree surgery.

Once you start passing on techniques to television viewers, you are wide open to criticism. Not everybody is going to approve. It goes with the territory. If you don't like the heat, stay out of the greenhouse. Or come down from the tree.

Ah yes, the world of trees. They're funny folk, the men of the trees. And the women. Loners most of them. Mavericks. Take a good look at a tree surgeon and you'll see an individualist with an interesting dress sense and a self-sufficient demeanour. It's almost as if being up there at a hundred feet, looking down on the rest of us, gives them a sort of privileged overview. Perhaps they see us mere mortal gardeners as the groundlings we really are.

I'm not being disparaging. Some of my best friends are tree surgeons. But you know what they say in Yorkshire: "They're all queer bar thee and me, and even tha's a bit queer." It's the Dales version of "There's nowt so queer as folk."

Anyway, back to my little problem. When I was at Kew, I was taught tree surgery by a handful of tree men and a man called George Brown. He was a lovely fella, George, and he wrote a book called *The Pruning of Trees, Shrubs and Conifers*, which became the standard work. It sits on a shelf in front of me. Signed. George died a good few years ago, but I, and a few hundred Kew students, remember him fondly and cherish the skills and experience he passed on to us.

Tree surgery has evolved a lot over the years. In the fifties they used to fill cavities created by rotten branches falling away from the trunk with concrete. In the late sixties we started using a type of polystyrene foam that expanded before your eyes and filled the hold completely so that water could find no entry.

Then it was decided that cavities were best left alone, filled with air as nature intended. I'm up with all this. But when it comes to limb removal, in my day we cut the limb flush with the trunk. In doing so, we'd avoid snags that could die back, and yet try to leave as small a cut surface as possible. Which is what I did with my birch tree on the telly.

I inadvertently unleashed the dogs of war. I had tree surgeons writing me tart notes about BS something-or-other, which says that we now cut off limbs just above the "knuckle" to leave the smallest cut surface possible, and how dare I go back to this prehistoric technique, which could lead to all sorts of problems with death and decay.

Well, I looked out over a garden of trees that had been pruned how George taught me 30 years ago. Clearly no one has told them that they should be unhappy and that they would have flourished far better if they had been treated to the new technique. I'm not averse to learning new tricks, but it does rattle me when old methods that have served generations of gardeners well are sneered at by those who never had to use them.

I wrote back to one of my critics, explaining my stance and suggesting that when the knuckle technique was consigned to the rubbish bin by the next generation he would know how I felt. To be fair, he did reply saying perhaps he had been a bit hasty.

My reason for mentioning all this is simply to reiterate my belief that gardening is not an exact science. There is more than one way of skinning a cat and removing a branch. It seems to me that the more experience you have, the more open minded you become. Which, I suppose, is my way of admitting that I'm getting older, and the older I get, the less certain I am that there is only one way of doing something.

So the next time you root a cutting using a technique that your granny taught you, don't be put off by some young tearaway who tells you the latest methods are better. Just smile, safe in the knowledge that the best way to do something is the way that works for you.

There, I feel better now.

2002

My Pet Theory

There really are no two ways about it, gardeners and pets do not, under any circumstances, go together. Oh, I know it is a picturesque sight when a Labrador snoozes in the sun on the lawn in summer, and when the cat curls up on top of the wall, but for 99 per cent of the time pets really are a pain to gardeners. I've had them all so I should know.

I do still have the dogs, but the only way to keep the garden looking decent is to keep them out of it, except when they are under strict control and made to lie down in the sun on the lawn in summer so that they look picturesque.

Our solution is to have a dog path leading up the side of the garden to the field, the theory being that this way they can't damage anything that really matters.

But what then do you do about the neighbours' dogs? They'll sneak into your garden when your back is turned and scarify your lawn with their claws. And if you are wondering why on earth your conifers are going brown at the bottom, it's as likely as not a case of the dreaded Alsatian cocklegicus.

But don't make the mistake of thinking that a cat will be an easier alternative. No fear. Cats are diggers and rollers and scratchers. Have you ever watched a cat relieving itself? First of all it excavates a hole. Next it relieves itself somewhere completely different. Then it scrapes back the earth on a third remote site. Three lots of damage for the price of one.

A cat will chew off your catmint when it is a small plant, or roll on it if it is large. It will scratch the bark of young trees to sharpen its claws and your pricey parrotia will undoubtedly perish prematurely.

You might also have noticed that cats never seem to go in their own gardens, always in somebody else's. It was Professor John Carey who noted that although it is an offence to climb your neighbour's fence and defecate among his vegetables, you can send a feline accomplice on precisely the same errand with impunity.

What about a budgie then? Nope. Not unless you want to be arrested. It would seem tempting to empty the budgie's cage into the garden, in the belief that the droppings will do the plants good. However what you will also deposit on your beds and borders is a lot of exotic seed. When the policeman with botanical aspirations spots that cannabis is growing among your French marigolds, he might not be convinced that your budgie, and not you, is to blame. Many's the old-age pensioner now serving time at Her Majesty's pleasure on account of their delightful pet budgie.

Hamsters and gerbils? Don't touch 'em with a barge pole. Their food is just as dodgy, packed with exotics that will run riot among your carefully planted summer bedding.

Ah, but what about a horse? Instant manure and all that. Have you seen the size of vets' bills, feeding bills, transportation bills and saddlery bills for a horse? You could buy a de luxe conservatory for what it costs you to keep a nag for a year.

So which pet can be relied on to be garden friendly? I have the answer. What you need is a goldfish. It doesn't matter whether it is a shubunkin or koi carp (except that koi carp cost an arm and a fin), but most importantly, a goldfish will never give you trouble in your garden, provided that you keep it in a tank indoors. Put it in your garden pool and you instantly attract herons which will spear them and leave you suicidal, especially if you have paid £3,000 for that special koi carp.

In a tank on the sideboard your goldfish will cause you no anguish. It will not eat your plants or soil your lawn and when, after a good thirty years or so, it shuffles off its mortal coil, you can take it from the tank and bury it in the garden. There, beneath some little bedding plant, it will rot down into fish-meal that you would normally have to go out and buy in a sack at the garden centre. The years of pleasure it gave you on the sideboard are matched by its feeding properties in the soil. Now that's what I call a pet with a purpose.

1994

Live and Let Live

Have you seen the shelves of chemicals in your local garden centre recently? Have you noticed how much smaller they have become? Oh, there's always lots of Grow-Like-Fury and Flower-Your-Head-Off, but there's a far smaller choice when it comes to Splat! And Kill Well. The chemical world is not what it was, thank goodness.

And yet there are still one or two gardeners who do not feel happy unless they spray their patch with noxious fluid at least once a week. Don't worry. I'm not launching into a tirade about the value of organic gardening. Well, I am, but not of the beat-you-about-the-head variety. It's all about mindset and changing the way we think about gardening. Oh glory, that sounds a bit evangelical.

Well, let me explain. I belong to the generation that grew up with a sprayer in one hand and a budding knife in the other. During my Parks Department apprenticeship, I was often sent out to buy stuff that had to be signed for in the poisons book at the local supplier. Presumably this was so that they could find out what you may have died of if they found you writhing in agony on the potting-shed floor. We sprayed healthy plants with evil-smelling fluid to keep them that way. We fumigated our greenhouses with fireworks that emitted noxious gas, or piles of nicotine shreds that had to be stamped out if the pile suddenly caught fire and burned merrily instead of smouldering and giving out its lethal smoke.

Our only protection on this terror-run was a hanky that could be held over your nose and mouth while you applied the right pressure with your welly: enough to quell flames, but not to put out the fire completely.

On one occasion I had previously used my hanky to test the direction of the wind. For this, I filled it with John Innes base fertiliser and shook it to see which way the fine particles drifted on the breeze. I would then know where to stand with my sprayer, so I didn't get my own back, so to speak.

And then, during the terror-run, I discovered the effects of base fertiliser coming in close proximity with eyes, nose and throat. This was more than unpleasant, but compared with a friend of mine, who suffered permanent damage from nicotine gas, I escaped lightly. And all so that our plants would be free of pests and diseases.

When viewed like this, it seems bonkers to even consider using products like these to keep our plants healthy while we suffer as a result. Our gardens may supply us with food as well as flowers, but it is not as if our race will die out if we stop producing high yields outside the back door. This is gardening, not farming.

That's why I think we need a different mindset nowadays. I am as much of a perfectionist as the next man when it comes to growing a good plant, such as the hole-free hosta or the greenfly-free rose. But at what price? I think we should stop expecting unreasonable idealism in our gardens.

If you walk along a hedge bank in May, what do you see? Red campion and cow parsley, bluebells and greater stitchwort, lush grasses and vetches, and you rejoice in its beauty. You do not notice the caterpillars that may be feeding there, or the blackfly.

And yet, when you walk along a flower border in your garden, you notice the slug damage on fat and juicy leaves, the colonies of greenfly on the young shoots of roses, the snail trail along the ground and the birds pecking at flower buds. So what are you, a gardener or a hypochondriac?

Oh, I know the illnesses of your plants are not imagined, but isn't it time you put them into perspective? Feed your soil with manure, garden compost and organic fertiliser, and it will grow plants better equipped to shrug off pests and diseases.

Grow resistant varieties: leathery-leaved roses are less likely to fall prey to mildew and blackspot, and there are disease-resistant strains of other plants, too. You don't need to grow

Michaelmas daisies that are martyrs to mildew, or potatoes that always get blight.

You can have trouble-free cops if you choose carefully, and you will enjoy your garden a lot more if you stop being paranoid. It may seem as if I am lowering my standards when I suggest that if you see a hosta leaf with a hole in it you move your deckchair a few feet away. But isn't this preferable to leaving slug pellets where they can damage more than just slugs?

A farmer I know was bemoaning the way gardeners put piles of slug pellets in their borders when he scatters them so they fall 18 inches apart. "Think of the savings," he said, "in terms of wildlife and pets as well as money." There are times when farmers can teach gardeners a bit about basic common sense.

2004

What's in a Name?

Every year in *The Times* there appears a list, drawn up from the classified pages throughout the year, of the top ten names bestowed on babies. The Alexanders and Henrys, the Sophies and Carolines retain their popularity year in, year out, but the names that seldom figure any more are those attached to flowers.

It is rare to find a baby girl christened Hyacinth, partly due, I suspect, to Miss Routledge's portrayal of the Bucket lady. The only name that seems to have survived is Rose which means, quite simply in the language of flowers, love.

You see, what people fail to appreciate is that flowers have a language all of their own. It is a tradition that began in the harems of the Ottoman Empire centuries ago when suitors would leave their love a flower rather than a note. The custom made its way to Britain in the nineteenth century and the Floral Code was born.

The moustache-adorned Victorian suitor would send his intended a suitable posy; the flowers selected for their accuracy of sentiment. Red roses meant "love", as did scarlet tulips, but there were other subtle messages, sent by beaux to their belles: a white lily signified purity, and a posy of violets modesty. It is, one surmises, a hopeful mother who christens her child Lily.

Hyacinth means play, to which there is little I can add, and Buttercup means ingratitude, which is clearly why it is applied to old cows. Nobody, to my knowledge, has ever christened their offspring Lobelia, though I have met one or two children for whom it would be especially fitting. It indicates malevolence.

Poppy does pop up from time to time. Probably when daddy wanted a boy; it means consolation. It is freely admitted that confusion did exist in this floral code, and that opinions varied as to the meanings of certain flowers. Call a daughter Paeony and you could be saddling her with either shyness or shame. Settle on Lavender and imply distrust or pleasant memories. Heather occurs now and again. It is rather suitable for an only child; it signifies solitude. But do let me warn you off even considering naming your daughter Marigold. It implies grief and daughters, they tell me, can give you plenty of that between the ages of one and fifty.

Perhaps floral names are most suited to country children. Pop Larkin, settled among the orchards and hop poles of Kent, bestowed upon his progeny the names of Petunia and Zinnia and Primrose. But when it came to his son it was Montgomery. Now why are men never called after flowers? There must be a bloom or two that a self-respecting chap would be happy to hide behind.

Johnny Cash may have met a boy called Sue, but I bet he never met one called Narcissus. Mr Pooter, in the Grossmith brothers' *Diary of a Nobody* did call his son Lupin, according to the floral code it denotes voraciousness, but nobody else has done.

I suppose Cosmo is almost cosmos and Tom is almost tomato but I'm stretching it a bit now. Unless, of course, men were to be named after vegetables rather than flowers. They are undeniably manly. After all, Albert R. Broccoli did produce the James Bond movies, and Jasper Carrott is a passable comedian. Surnames, I know, so it's cheating. Perhaps a sensitive British parent will always baulk at naming its child after something that can also be found on a plate: Harry, Lee, Cal and Art are never likely to be used as diminutive forms of Haricot, Leek, Calabrese and Artichoke.

But hang on a moment, I've found it. The vegetarian man's name, it's Basil. And I bet that crops up as often as Hyacinth in the births columns of *The Times*.

1995

Mum

There comes a time in every chap's life when he has to grow up. Oh, he can pretend he's grown up and generally carry himself responsibly as far as outward appearances go, but there is a moment when he knows that he really has reached the age of maturity. It happens when he loses his last parent.

In December my mum, having battled with rheumatoid arthritis for 30-odd years, finally succumbed to a stroke and pneumonia. She was 78. My dad died back in 1986. They'd been a devoted pair, happier in each other's company than anyone else's. Mum's world fell apart, but she gritted her teeth, became even more bloody-minded about her complaint, and tried as best she could to get on with life. It wasn't easy. Three replacement joints, the removal of several toes, and deformed hands that could only hold a mug with a large handle were bad enough. Then walking became more difficult. In the last couple of years she could not stand up unaided. But still she smiled, sometimes, in between the tears.

My love of the great outdoors came from her. She would never sit in a room without a window open and preferably a door. When she finally moved into a nursing home they found her a ground-floor room with a door that opened on to the drive. She could watch comings and goings and sit there, with a woolly wrap over her shoulders, in the chilliest weather. "I don't like being fast," she would say, meaning I don't like to be shut in.

When we were small, that gnarled and crooked little body was upright and slender, like a willow wand. She had wonderful hands. Even to the end her nails were beautifully manicured, but I never remember her wearing gloves for gardening. She would sow seeds and dig the vegetable patch. She would shout warnings whenever our careering bicycles looked like demolishing some treasure: a patch of nasturtiums, her father's favourite sweet Williams, or the hydrangea on the corner. "Mind the Lone Ranger," she would shout, as our bicycles brushed past its fleshy leaves.

Because of mum's claustrophobia, and I suppose that's what it was, we were outdoors in all but the foulest weather. With my sister Kath in the pushchair and me holding on to the handle, we would walk for miles, down by the River Wharfe among cow parsley and meadow cranesbill, through waist-high bluebells in Middleton Woods, or breasting the bracken and trampling the heather on Ilkley Moor.

When I was nine I had to make a collection of dried and pressed wildflowers as a school project. We travelled up and down the dales in search of rarities, as you were allowed to pick them then, and mum would triumphantly identify them with the aid of a wildflower book from the local library. "I think this is evergreen alkanet," she declared. There it sits to this day, crisp and flat, with my own spidery writing identifying it as such. I won first prize, five shillings, which bought me *The Observer's Book of Wild Animals*. But it was really down to my mum.

When I said that gardening was what I wanted to do for a living, and that I wanted to leave school at 15 before I took my O-levels, they must have been worried. But apart from a few sideways looks at one another they didn't show it. Instead my dad made enquiries and landed me a job at the local nursery. I'd found my place in the world and I think they knew it.

In later life, when gardening became impossible for my mum, she still insisted on a window-box filled with small spring-flowering bulbs, followed by summer bedding, then winter-flowering pansies. I never heard her utter a Latin name; she wasn't that kind of gardener. To her, gardening was instinctive. She seemed to have been born knowing how to take a cutting and sow a seed.

When I started to go to night school, I'd come back and tell her when she was doing something wrong. "Oh, I see," she'd say, and carry on doing what she'd always done. To my teenage annoyance her ways, although not "proper", would produce results. Her reasoning was that if something worked for her that's the way she would do it. I learnt the lesson.

I know that she was proud of me, because she told me so. Her ultimate compliment, on enjoying one of my programmes, would be to say that it was magnificent. It might have been slightly over the top, but I never demurred. When asked if she was any relation to me, she would draw herself up to her full five feet and a bit, and say, "I'm 'is mum."

But my favourite story of all concerns her hairdresser, Guy. As well as tending to my mum's hair, which was dark to the end and never dyed, he was also patronised by the Duchess of Devonshire on her visits to Bolton Abbey. I've met the Duchess on several occasions and we've always got on. One day, as Guy was drying my mum's hair, he said, "The Duchess of Devonshire was asking after you." Mum's hearing was the one thing that never deserted her. But on this occasion, for the benefit of all the other ladies in the salon, some of whom were under dryers, she said, "I'm sorry, you'll have to speak up. What did you say?" He replied, at volume. "The Duchess of Devonshire was asking after you!" Mum smiled, confident that the message had now been heard by all. "Oh, that's nice."

She was, like all mums, a bit special, and I count my blessings that she had the wisdom to let me follow her into the garden. I will always miss her.

2003

MAY

Sitting Pretty

When the first warming rays of sun strike your back doorstep your thoughts will doubtless turn to sitting out. Now that's something we gardeners don't do nearly enough. Sit still. If you'd have caught me thirty-odd years ago sitting on our back doorstep I'd have had a slice of bread and dripping in my hand. But those days are gone. Nowadays the doctors warn of the dangers of sitting on a cold stone doorstep, and the health food experts tell us not to eat dripping.

But sitting is something I recommend. First, however, you must find your seat. Mind you, have you taken a look at garden furniture lately? Do you have an existing mortgage? Do you really want a second mortgage? Judging by the price of some garden furniture you'd think the stuff was better sold at Sotheby's.

In fact some of it is. Auction houses now hold sales of garden architecture (including seats) in their lavish country premises in places like Billingshurst in Sussex. Here a man will knock down to you a garden bench (though he'll probably have a flash name for it like "Coalbrookdale cast iron seat embellished with swags of nasturtiums").

Have one if auntie has left you a legacy; if she hasn't you'll have to nip down to the garden centre and invest more lightly (but not much) in their array of recliners.

Now I have had something of a battle on my hands lately. My favourite steamer chair (Heal's several years ago, under £100) is frowned upon by the memsahib.

It's wooden and I've acquired some Indian kelim cushions to pad it a bit. Very Vita Sackville-West. But the lady wife is not enamoured. The thing is at the wrong angle (she says) and the cushions are prickly. She turns them upside down and sits on the corduroy material because she finds the kelim side prickly.

There am I, tastefully arranging my garden furniture so that it's redolent of Sissinghurst, and now all I get is a plaintive plea for one of those nice white plastic recliners on wheels that don't trap your fingers and can be moved around the garden easily. Apparently, the fringed, striped cushion is very comfortable.

I've told her that Vita and Harold would have died rather than have white plastic seats but she's adamant. Mind you, there's not much chance of her calling me Hadji either.

When I asked her if she'd mind wearing jodhpurs, lace-up boots, a belted jacket and a picture hat she looked positively frosty, standing there in her tracksuit and Reeboks. "Sometimes," she says, "comfort must come before style."

That's not something that ever entered my head when I sat on the doorstep eating bread and dripping . . .

1991

Whatever the Weather

Gardeners, perhaps more than other folk, are completely at the mercy of the weather. We battle on, through rain and hail, snow and fog, gale-force winds and scorching sun. Well, most of the time. There are days when even the most dedicated son or daughter of the soil has to throw in the trowel and call it a day. Oh, we moan about it, as much as the rest of the population, but there is one vital difference between us and them. We know we can't control the weather. They expect to be able to.

Take last winter, when we had that snowfall. You'd have thought Armageddon had arrived. It interrupted journeys. It stopped some people from getting to work. Well, I mean, it shouldn't happen should it? They should be able to do something about it, shouldn't they?

Don't get me wrong. I'm as critical as the next guy of feeble excuses peddled by government departments and local councils for failure to keep roads open or trains running, when the real answer is sloppy management. But when it comes to controlling the weather, I'm glad we can't do it.

For decades, the population has been given to understand that nothing can or must stand in the way of man and his quest for personal freedom. If a chap wants to travel from A to B in a given time, he should be able to. Nothing should prevent this, and anything that does is an infringement of his liberty. Even foul weather. If you think I'm joking, just look at the indignation of people who get stuck in their cars in snowdrifts. There is a limit to the effects of a gritting lorry.

I am the first person to sympathise with the victims of flooding. Nothing can be worse than seeing your house and your treasures submerged in foul black slime. But at the risk of inspiring hatred in all those who live on low-lying land near rivers that are prone to bursting their banks, it's the most natural thing in the world. It may not be convenient. There are times when it is tragic, but it is still natural.

Humans tend to forget sometimes that we are just one cog in the large and complicated mechanism of life. I blame it on mobile phones, the internet and the media, just as our grandparents used to blame it on the rockets that were sent up into space. But I think I have more grounds to do so. I blame it on technology and the media because they've raised expectations to an unreasonable level. They have led us to believe that we are the sole reason for the existence of the planet and that, in time, anything is achievable. Modern technology is so complex and far-fetched that to control the activities of the heavens seems simple in comparison. But it isn't, is it? I find that rather reassuring.

It does man good to feel small. Any gardener knows that. Anyone who has sown a seed or watched a plant grow knows that man can help nature but can't govern it. That in itself can have dire consequences; one prime reason that George Bush wanted to go to war with Iraq speedily was because the weather was right. It makes you think. Yet, for most of the time, in spite of late frosts that damage fruit blossom, and summer bedding that dries to a crisp due to drought, we learn to rub along with nature. And so we should.

When nature flexes her muscles, man is reminded that he is not all powerful and all controlling. On the contrary, he is still at the mercy of the elements and would do well to be a bit more respectful of them. I'm getting all pompous now, aren't I? Better shut up and get on with the weeding. But when next you are out in the garden, pottering under a blue sky, while the birds are singing and the bees are buzzing, just stop for a while and savour the moment.

Then reflect on the fact that it may be foul weather that inspires newspaper editorials, but it's fair weather that inspires the gardener and leaves him with feelings that he'll never forget. Funny really.

All those front-page stories only ever go on about tempest and flood, snow and ice. "Britain grinds to a halt," they scream, and "The big freeze." Then the thaw comes and it's all forgotten. Just like childhood, when it is the best and brightest of days that stick in your memory, so it is with gardening. But don't hold your breath. You'll never read a headline, "Lovely day: millions out in the garden enjoying themselves."

We may have been warned about global warming, the rising seas and shrinking continents, but one thing is certain: there has always been weather, and it's always unpredictable. A bit like man really.

2003

The Kitchen Project

There is a poem I remember from my youth that runs: "I want a kitchen garden, with box to line the routes, where things go soft and harden, and cling to people's boots." I even remember the author – Daniel Pettiward. There were other lines like, "I want to be surrounded by bone manure and bees," and "pippin blossom breaking into the potting shed." They are all wonderful images, to be conjured up by the fireside in winter when I am making plans for the rosy future of my garden. A kitchen garden figures in them largely.

I have one at the moment, but if I were honest I would have to admit that it is more kitchenette than kitchen. Scullery even. It is tiny. But it does have "box to line the routes," even if the run that entirely surrounds it is no more than 50ft or so (divide that by four and you'll see just how small my kitchen garden is).

Not that it is a rectangle. It is actually two triangles, simply because the view from the kitchen window, up the path that separates these two beds, terminates in a peeling, tapered white beehive of the WBC type. (I've always thought it odd that one of the most romantic structures on earth – the beehive – has been given such resolutely unromantic names by beekeepers. Take your pick from WBS – named after its "inventor", William Braughton Carr – National and Improved Langstroth.

Ah, where has the old "skep" gone?) The two triangular beds frame my beehive.

But I have in mind a larger scheme that will sit in front of the greenhouse, slightly to the left of the beehive. From the moment this germ of an idea appeared I have been mulling over the disadvantages of kitchen gardens. I know all the advantages – fresh produce, great flavour, the sense of satisfaction – after all, I've written about them often enough encouraging other folk to have a go. But what about the downside? Well, have you ever seen a photograph in a big glossy book showing a kitchen garden in November? Or even between November and March? No. And why? Because kitchen gardens are things of beauty only between April and October.

So the challenge, to myself, is to make sure my kitchen garden is beauteous in winter, too, which is why, no doubt, the world and his wife bring box hedges into play.

There is, you will admit, nothing inspiring about an allotment in winter. It becomes a neglected sea of dripping Brussels sprout tops and bolted cabbages, however assiduous the owner. That rolling main of fresh-dug soil is of limited appeal. What a gardener wants is greenery – and plenty of it.

So what I shall do is divide my kitchen garden up into small beds. I will try to be a little more imaginative in my inclusion of the aforesaid greenery, without turning my plot into a patchwork quilt of lurid *Euonymus fortunei* 'Emerald 'n' Gold' and *Choisya ternata* 'Sundance'. My sensibilities could not cope with that. Mmm. Looks like box then, with yew finials. Well, I could do worse.

The pattern will be everything, but I think I'll keep it simple – a rectangle on each side, divided into four by grass paths, knowing that if they wear badly in their first year I shall have to replace them with stone. Note to self: make grass paths same width as stone slabs so that replacement will be easier.

On a whim, I ran my plan past my youngest daughter yesterday afternoon. She came out of the house to enquire why I was gazing vacantly into space. I suppose this sort of contemplation gives new meaning to the phrase 'lost the plot'.

I explained that, being a bear of little brain, I have to look at things long and hard before I can come to a conclusion. She seemed to approve. Now I have to get it past the lady of the house. This potential Arcadia of All Things Culinary is immediately opposite the kitchen sink, and while I have no wish to imply that my wife is lashed to it for most of the day, I would be being economical with the truth if I did not admit that she is familiar with that particular location.

For that reason I will promise her cut flowers as well as vegetables. She has a fondness for dahlias that is rather admirable, fostered by a visit to Chatsworth last summer. I fear she may be setting her sights a little high. I will also try to fit in some handsome fruit bushes. Standard gooseberries perhaps, and a few step-over apple trees. My wife does like her fruit, but she also likes it (along with her vegetables) to appear freshly washed and trimmed on the draining board, rather than completely coated with mud, foliage intact, in a rather picturesque trug basket, which used to be my way of delivering the greengrocery.

You'll see from this run-down that my project is very much at the formative stages. So if you ever come here and see two little triangular beds with a beehive between them, you'll know I bottled out, and that, as yet, my kitchen garden remains a figment of my imagination. But I'll get the bone manure and bees in somewhere, and the pippin blossom is only a stone's throw from the potting shed.

2006

The Hole Truth

So far I have managed to fool everybody into thinking that I am a proper gardener, but now it can be revealed. I am a fraud. What is the one gardening activity guaranteed to sort the wheat from the chaff and define a true gardener? Digging, that's what. And I confess that I am no digger.

Pull from your bookshelf that old gardening tome and among its dusty pages you will find intricate diagrams of freshly turned soil and symmetrical trenches as deep as a municipal main drain. Here are engravings of men able to perform something akin to the art of open-cast mining in a waistcoat, tie and trilby, while still having enough breath left to puff away at a pipe of shag tobacco.

Beneath the instructive step-by-step operations carried out by this human earth mover are such delightful words as spit, tilth and farmyard manure. What's more, these excavations are clearly carried out in a garden entirely constructed from freshly sieved soil. He may well have grown wonderful parsnips as a result of his hard labour but, quite frankly, I'd sooner live on lettuce.

Funny really, because I actually like digging. A bit. It's a satis-fying sort of operation but it does need to be done in easy stages and, in my garden, that's where the difficulty lies. The soil is either stony, well flinty to be precise, or the stuff that isn't flint is chalky or root ridden, and the whole lot is pretty well compacted. From this you will gather that at Barleywood there are no easy stages. I can state this without any fear of contradiction because I have just come in from a short, sharp stint at digging and can still feel the numbness across the small of my back.

Now if you are one of those resourceful people who has just invented a novel earth mover that simply flips up the soil and allows it to do a double axle and triple toe-loop before falling back into the hole, weeds down, please do not bother to write to me. I am one of those odd bods who, when he does dig, likes to use a proper wooden-handled spade which is well-balanced and has a sharp blade. I will derive no pleas-ure at all from poking at my soil with something that looks as though it might once have been used for bear-baiting in the Middle Ages.

I can often be found digging with a fork, rather than a spade, simply because there is more chance of getting the prongs of the fork down between my flints than there is of penetrating with the entire length of the spade blade. I only stand a chance of digging down to anything like a full spit of a spade on my much cultivated vegetable plot. In this circumstance I can see why digging is such a joy. It is the purest of pleasures to culti-vate an allotment which has earth the colour of soot and the texture of John Innes potting compost. To compare this with digging in the rest of my garden is like comparing the singing of Maria Callas with that of a ginger tom.

For this reason I have developed a system of earth cultivation, unlike that found in Victorian or Edwardian books, which is just as effective.

Instead of taking out a trench and barrowing the earth to the other end of the plot, I simply push in my spade or fork and throw the soil forward to create a much shallower trench. I line this trench with well-rotted garden compost, or manure if possible, and then I throw more soil forward on top of the enrichment. When the job is finished, I spread more manure on the top of the freshly turned soil.

This way the soil ends up being cultivated to a depth of around 23cm (9in), which is ample for most perennials and bedding plants, and the manure or compost is near the surface which is where it is needed when plants are young. If I need to plant a tree or a shrub, I dig a deeper hole just where it is needed. Parsnips and carrots are grown in raised beds of sieved soil supported by old floorboards.

I have never double dug in my life, except for an examination, and I firmly believe that none of my plants is any the worse for it. There is no earthly reason why soil in flower-beds and borders should be dug over after this initial cultivation. A light pricking over with a fork in spring is enough to relieve compaction and surface mulching with plenty of organic matter allows the worms to mix the stuff in for you.

Purists may believe that there's nothing to beat a bit of good old double digging, but show me a double digger and I'll show you someone with back trouble.

1998

Garden of Delights

A couple of weeks ago, I was asked if I would contribute to a book called *Delights*, based on a volume of the same title that JB Priestley wrote many years ago. In that original anthology, Priestley, author of *The Good Companions* et al, included small vignettes on things in life that he found particularly pleasing.

It set me thinking about some of my own. Afternoon tea, for instance with Lapsang and seed cake. Retired admirals. Church bells. Rowing boats. But these have no specific connections with the garden, so here I should confine my delight to those that can be found just outside my back door.

I won't include plants as such, otherwise this would be no more than a list of favourites, from roses to agapanthus, hostas to primroses. So I'll try to be a bit more inventive.

Garden gates seem a good starting point. Not just those that are aesthetically pleasing, but those that run easily on their hinges. There is nothing more likely to get you into a bate than a garden gate with a broken hinge or a stiff catch. By the time you've passed through, your temper has been tested, the skin knocked from your knuckles and you'll need to calm yourself down before you can take in the view, however delightful. But a well-balanced gate, that opens with a satisfying click or clang on the catch, then swings easily and silently open, is a wonderful introduction to a garden.

May

Some of my garden tools qualify as delights. Take my border fork. I've had it for 20 years or more and it was old when I got it. As a result, the prongs are needle sharp and the whole implement is light and easily wielded, with a shaft as smooth as silk.

Then there's my budding knife. It's the one I was given on my first day at work, 45 years ago. 'The Burbank' it says on the side. They don't make them any more. I cherish it still, take cuttings with it and use it when I'm tying things up. It sits neatly in my hand, but then the two of them have been together for a long time now. If I ever lost it, I'd be desolate, but one generous viewer provided me with an identical replacement a few years ago, so that I can use the 'stand-in' rather than risking the original.

My cat, Spud, delights me. Especially now that he's older and doesn't catch birds like he used to. He qualifies since he's always around me, jumping up onto my back when I'm bending down, tending to some plant or other. He did it on camera back in my *Gardeners' World* days, when I was planting potatoes. I know full well that nobody took a blind bit of notice of what I was saying, they were all so busy cooing over the cat.

Weather vanes are always a delight. Across the way, the usual cockerel swings to and fro atop the church spire, but on the roof of my barn, I have a hoe leaning on a watering can and pointing in the direction of today's gust. I made a cardboard cut-out of the design 20-odd years ago and took it to the local blacksmith, who replaced it with the same in blackened steel. I see it from the window as I write – the wind is in the north-west. It's comforting, somehow, to know ...

Beehives and bell jars qualify. Traditional, white-painted beehives I have always used as garden ornaments, their design is so pleasing. Bell jars I use on the veg patch in the early spring, coaxing on a few lettuces ahead of the rest. Underneath the crystal domes, they take on the appearance of prize specimens, and I have to steel myself to cut and eat them.

Tadpoles are a delight. First the full stops, then the commas, then those little black leeches that turn into marbles with tails, and finally the frogs themselves. I don't need exotic, brightly coloured lizards and chameleons, my frogs and toads and newts will do me nicely. Their understated beauty is what delights.

Smooth, round pebbles delight, gravel irritates (especially when stuck in the treads of my shoes). Watering cans delight, hoses annoy, especially when they tangle themselves with no help from me.

Bird baths delight thanks to the antics of the bathers, and so do nut feeders hung from trees.

But the biggest delight of them all is the lark, which sings on high in a clear blue sky. I hear it first in early March, and the challenge is to spot it. High up it soars, singing its heart out without pausing for breath. How can it do so, since it must need so much energy just to stay aloft? There is triumph in pin-pointing that black speck up in the blue, and then in watching it swoop to earth and disappear in the short grass of the meadow.

These are the delights of being out in the open air, and nothing would induce me to trade them for those indoors.

2009

If At First You Don't Succeed . . .

I have high hopes that by the time you read this I will have had a vintage wisteria year. Right now, the two that occupy the front of our house are simply awash with buds but, oh, the heartache it has taken to get this far.

When we moved here five years ago, there was an old and venerable beauty clambering across the brickwork, courtesy of an assortment of wires. But it was clearly on its last legs. Now, wisterias last a good many years – well into three figures – and this one had a trunk that was a good 25cm in diameter. But two-thirds of that diameter was hollow – rotten. I knew the plant would probably limp on for another three or four years, but by then it really would be past it.

I decided to bite the bullet and rip out the old one and replace it with two youngsters. Our house looks like a classic doll's house, with the front door in the middle and two windows on either side on both the ground and first floors. It has what an architectural historian would call 'five bays'. It is Georgian and constructed out of mellow local brick with a clay tile roof, and the front faces south-west. Wisteria suited it, and I felt there was room for a brace.

So with a heavy heart and a sharp mattock, I chopped out the old plant, secure in the knowledge that at least our tall hedge would hide my destructive activity from the neighbours. An hour's work and then it was no more. The brickwork was bare, and there was enough fresh ground beneath the wall to put two young wisterias back without planting in the same patch of soil. The only question was which variety?

I've always loved plain old *Wisteria sinensis*, with its lilac-purple flowers, but decided in the end that the house could take the long-tasselled *Wisteria floribunda* 'Multijuga', whose flower trails are 60–90cm long – a decision influenced, I admit, by the fact that there were two handsome 2m-tall, pot-grown specimens in my local garden centre. I bought them home, I enriched the soil, I planted them and tied them in.

Now, the most frequently asked gardening question of all time is "how do I get my wisteria to flower?" The answer is always the same. It needs a sunny wall (south or west facing), and it needs pruning twice a year, shortening unwanted long growths to about 30cm in July and then cutting back all side-shoots to finger length in January. A decent helping of rose fertiliser in February and again in June will also help. Do all those things and it should flower well.

But there's one other caveat – your wisteria should be a grafted plant. If it has been propagated by grafting, then the scion (or upper section) will be of proven flowering quality. If it has been propagated by layering it may well be "flower shy", and no amount of coaxing will ever get it to produce a massive show of blooms. You can spot a grafted plant by looking for the graft union (a sort of knobbly junction) several centimetres above soil level.

I looked at my plants in the garden centre. They had been grafted. So in they went and in the first year, not surprisingly, there was no sign of a flower, but they did produce plenty of shoots that I could tie in and help to cover the wall. They must have grown 2m or more.

In their second year, I had a couple of flower trails and 3m of growth. In their third year the left-hand plant started to look a bit yellow (we are overlying chalk) and produced no flowers at all. I worried. And fed it. And told myself that at least the right-hand plant seemed happy. The next year the same thing happened.

By the end of last year, the total coverage of the wall was impressive, and I had to cut plenty of growth out of the gutters. Only about 2m in the centre of the house, above the door, has not yet been covered with stems. By the end of this summer, coverage will be complete.

But the lack of flowering still worried me. As did the yellow foliage on the left-hand plant. But by the end of last summer it didn't look quite as chlorotic, so the fertiliser I had fed it must have helped.

I am also very assiduous about my pruning. I can get most of the long shoots off in summer by leaning out of bedroom windows (though not the ones right at the top), but the plants get a proper going over with the help of an extending ladder in January, when new stems are tied in where needed and others are cut back to the length of a finger.

And, at long last, I have been rewarded. I checked the plants this morning and was astounded by the number of flower buds. You can always tell them from leaf and stem buds because they are fatter and covered in down. Both plants are awash and I am totally over-excited.

So if you are planning a new wisteria, be patient. Plant a grafted one against a sunny wall, space out and tie in the stems as they grow, prune it twice a year and feed it, too. Your patience will be rewarded and you will have those elegant, fragrant flower trails in spring.

Of course, by the time you are reading this, we could have had a late frost and I will be rending my shirt and investing in sackcloth and ashes. But then, at least I know my plants are capable of flowering. And there is always next year . . .

2008

A Magical Tale

Fantasy, that's the name of the game. If you want to get ahead, get an imagination. I mean, look at the success of *Harry Potter* and *The Lord of the Rings*. Critics have fallen hungrily on such offerings, being quick to explain that there is a raging appetite within the population for books and films to take us out of ourselves and into a parallel world that's peopled by witches, wizards and hobbits.

Of course, it's all made up. There is no real danger of you ever walking round the end of your garden shed and bumping into a dementor. Neither are you likely to encounter Gandalf in your gooseberry patch. And anyway, such encounters in your garden would be far less fantastical than the reality of the things that are happening there already.

You don't believe me? Let me explain. Once upon a time, there was an interfering meddler called The Gardener, who decided that Mother Nature was far too slack in her approach. He began to examine her children and found them to be wanting in many areas.

One of the children that caught his eye was the chrysanthemum. Now Mother Nature had decided that what she wanted from her chrysanthemum was a bit of colour just when all her other children were getting tired and dowdy. As a result, the chrysanthemum obligingly flowered in autumn.

What a waste, thought The Gardener. Flowers that are so beautiful and so long lasting should be available all year round, not just in the autumn. So The Gardener worked out a way of cheating the chrysanthemum into thinking that autumn had arrived before it really had, by making the days shorter and the nights longer. All it took was a piece of black polythene. And if it wanted to flower too soon, it could be dissuaded from doing so if its days were made longer by hanging light bulbs over it.

Lovely. The Gardener could now have chrysanthemums all year round. Emboldened by this success he decided to try other spells. The poinsettia, that wonderful Christmas flower, really should be kept for Christmas, but was there any way in which the plant could be improved?

Ah yes, of course. It is rather too tall for our modern rooms. Leave a poinsettia to its own devices, condoned by Mother Nature, and it will grow taller than a man. It would be much more useful only a foot or so tall. So The Gardener mixed up a potion in his cauldron and watered it on to the poinsettia, which then grew no more than a foot tall. The Gardener called this magical brew a growth retardant.

The Gardener enjoyed this new-found power and looked for other ways in which he could improve on Mother

Nature. He looked at more of her flowers, all the ones that filled her summer garden. They were beautiful, yes, but they could be so much more beautiful if they had even more petals. After all, the more petals they have, the more colour there is.

The Gardener busied himself among the flowers, mixing up the pollen and selecting the progeny until all the blooms in his garden were double. What colour he had now. What a wonderful and brilliant show.

So loudly did The Gardener sing with joy that he hardly noticed little else was singing. The birds were silent. They had all gone away, because the insects on which they fed no longer crawled and flew around the garden looking for nectar. It had all gone. Double flowers have no room for nectaries.

With the birds gone and the bees no longer humming among the flowers, another band of insects began to move in. These were the greenflies and the blackflies and the whiteflies who are happiest feeding on plants when there is little danger of them being eaten themselves. They are not interested in pollen, only sap, which is a wonderful breeding ground for viruses.

The Gardener noticed their arrival and knew he had to do something about it. He sat over his cauldron once more and cooked up some potions to kill the nasty insects that fed on his plants. Until more nasty insects flew in the next day. So The Gardener had to keep mixing and spraying, and mixing and spraying, until he was exhausted. Remember the Magic Porridge Pot?

But he did have a garden that was full of plants that would flower all year round, and which were nice and short so that he could look down on them, and which were full of double flowers for wonderful colour. And it was all such an improvement on what Mother Nature had grown in the first place. Wasn't it?

Fantasy worlds? They're not nearly as scary as the real thing.

2002

JUNE

The Mower You Wish For

One man went to mow, and mow, and mow . . . It seems to me that all I do at this time of year is cut the grass. Yes. I like the smell of new-mown hay, and yes the velvety greensward sets off the rest of the garden to perfection, but it doesn't half take a long time if you have a lot of lawn.

Perhaps I should look at alternatives. After all, grass is not the only surface that's suitable for sitting on. What about good old versatile concrete? One sheet of that and all my worries would be at an end. I could attractively texture it before it 'goes off' with a stiff broom. Mmm. Not really enough colour.

Well then, what about some of those stone slabs offered by the local garden centre? A friend strolled down my garden with me this weekend and told me that he intends to 'liven up' his landscape by making a stepping-stone path of coloured slabs from the top of the garden to the bottom. His garden is a good fifth of a mile long and nestles in a leafy backwater that boasts of being the largest cul-de-sac in Surrey. Did I success-fully disguise my wince at the prospect of this 'Wizard of Oz' walkway soon to be inflicted on the commuter belt? Not so much 'follow the yellow brick road' as 'follow the yellow and pink and green and brown flag path'. Perhaps not.

York stone is more subtle. It's also more expensive. If you're not careful you can run into three figures per square yard for rectangular dressed York stone. And if you're not equally careful, you're liable to acquire a nasty hernia when you come to lay it.

Perhaps I should look at alternative growing surfaces. "Why not an attractive chamomile lawn?" enquires a book on my shelves. Nice thought. I had a chamomile seat once and that was enough. Don't get me wrong; it was delicious and I intend to have another one soon, but it was by no means light on labour. It had to be hand weeded – lawn weedkillers kill chamomile. It had to be well watered in dry spells. I had to clip it by hand, with shears. And it died in a hard frost one winter.

Thyme is hardier, but the weeding and the clipping still need to be done. Alright, so you can use a rotary mower if you take care to set it high enough, but one false swipe and you've a nasty bare patch.

Perhaps gravel would be a better bet. It's cheap to buy, it's easy to lay over firmed earth, it keeps down weeds and it looks good. You can hear the burglars as they approach the house, too. I just wish the stuff wouldn't get stuck in between the ridges on the soles of my shoes. I find myself picking stray pebbles off the carpet all day.

You know, suddenly I've developed this soft spot for grass. Where's my mower . . .

1991

Wear and Tear

You know, when it comes to fashion, gardeners lag miles behind the rest of the population. There are people who spend hours musing over their wardrobe each morning. Will it be the bootleg trousers or the mini-skirt? The Levi's 501s or the chinos? Will the Prada bag be slung casually over the shoulder or would the Dolce & Gabbana carrier be more fitting with my outfit today?

If the language of fashion is as obscure to you as an Ancient Greek text, I apologise, but I do think we should consider more carefully what we wear in the garden to give this illustrious pastime just a tad more street cred.

Most folk, let's face it, treat the garden as some kind of scrapyard, if their wardrobe is anything to go by. A sweater that would be considered too tatty to give to the Oxfam shop is thought good enough to wear outdoors when you're turning the soil or deadheading the dahlias. Why is this so?

Oh, I can see that it makes sense to wear something old when you're pruning the roses, in case the thorns make a grab for your clothing. It is, I admit, foolhardy to approach a hybrid tea with secateurs in hand and cashmere on back. But that, surely, is an exception. The rose pruning season is a short one, and most gardeners can polish off all their bushes in half a day. Why is it, then, that they go around looking like Compo from *Last of the Summer Wine* the rest of the time from April to September?

Leaf through most classy magazines and you will discover that there is no shortage of smart leisure wear especially designed for the garden. You will see ladies from the county set, or at least that's what they look like, wearing Hermès scarves and sporting quilted jackets and pleated tweed skirts.

I've never been drawn to pleated skirts myself, in spite of a letter from one male reader some time ago who seriously exhorted me to wear a skirt in the garden. I kid you not. He matter-of-factly informed me that unless I had tried wearing one for all those strenuous jobs, I had yet to discover the most comfortable garment of all and that men should throw caution to the wind and give the skirt a chance.

I know the Scotsmen discovered the truth of this remark some years ago, but I am an Englishman and there is about as much likelihood of me slipping into a skirt as there is of Tony Blair trying on a toga. One gust of wind and my entire credentials would be open to ridicule.

Then we come to footwear. Time was when wellies were black and feet were damp. Then along came jolly green Hunter boots with buckles. The artisans sneered at them as something only suitable for those ladies in Fulham who take their children to school in a four-wheel drive vehicle. Not me. This is the one extravagance I will not be without. Even if the Fulham ladies may only wear them as a fashion statement, I know that in winter when my feet are encased in them all day long, week in, week out, I still have two things that pass for feet at the end of my legs and not two soggy lumps of flesh that look like poached cod.

I now possess a fine pair of buckled wellies that are lined with neoprene like a wet-suit, the ultimate luxury, and my feet stay warm and dry whatever the weather. However, as yet, I have not gone along with the latest fashion and plumped for dark blue ones. Well, it seemed pointless after the change of government.

When it comes to the rest of my body, I am a jeans man. On top of that I either wear a T-shirt in high summer, a checked lumberjack shirt or a sweatshirt in moderate weather, and one of three, thick, Peruvian sweaters that I bought in a craft shop when the weather turns really cold. The only trouble is that if it turns wet as well, the latter do begin to smell like a sodden yak, not that I've ever got near enough to a sodden yak to be sure.

The one thing I do insist on is clean clothing. Call me an old fusspot if you like, but I do like my linen crisp and my woollens soft, my jeans freshly washed and my socks sweet smelling. Or I did, until *Gardeners' World* came along. Carrying on the tradition set by my mother when I worked in the council nursery and turned up for work each Monday in clean clothes, I tried to do the same for the telly.

But it wouldn't wash. "You look far too clean," wailed the producers. As a result, the jeans I wear are last week's. They like a bit of mud on their jeans for authenticity, do the BBC. So far I have managed to appear grubby just by working in them for the week before they appear on screen. I shall start to worry when a make-up lady is brought in to distress them. But then those ladies in Fulham have probably been doing that for years.

1998

Joining the Rotary Club

Sadly, I think I'm beginning to lose it. You see, I've always hated rotary washing lines, as *Ground Force* viewers well know. I mean, there you are designing a garden with flowing lines and carefully judged planting, and then in the middle of it all this umbrella-like arrangement of spokes and cables pops up, from which drip shirts, vests, socks and knickers. Now who wants to look at that?

"It's alright for you," I can hear Mrs T now, burbling on about the practicalities of life. About how a tumble-dryer is not nearly as efficient as fresh air, and how the clothes smell so much better when they have been hung out to dry in the garden, rather than confined to a topsy-turvy life in that rumbling thing inside the boiler cupboard at the end of the kitchen.

I can see her point. I do love the scent of a freshly dried cotton shirt that has been divested of its moisture outdoors. The trouble is, while the process is happening I have to gaze on this unsightly whirligig contraption swathed in cotton and polyester. So I have resisted her entreaties so far at the new house, and bought her the tumble-dryer that sits in the aforementioned cupboard.

But last week I was away for a few days. When I returned, I walked across the orchard grass to feed the chickens. I had my eyes to the ground, bent double under the weight of the watering can that I was carrying to top up their drinker. It was from this hunched position that I saw it: the tell-tale hollow galvanised tube sunk into the ground.

I let out a strangled cry and looked across at the kitchen window, where Mrs T watched me, shaking her head. She came out of the back door. "You're losing your touch," she said. "Bill said you would spot it within 20 minutes. It's taken you an hour." I then saw the folded-up umbrella leaning against the wall.

"That seemed like the best place for it," she continued. "I can't dry washing in the shade, it needs sun and breezes. We thought it wouldn't look too bad there." Notice the use of the word we, intended to spread the blame on to Bill, our man what does. I harrumphed, a bit like Lord Emsworth's gardener Angus McAllister would harrumph in PG Wodehouse's wonderful Blandings novels. I mean, once the deed has been done, what can a chap do?

I had to stop and reflect that it could have been worse. The last *Ground Force* garden I made was on the Isle of Sheppey, where they run their washing lines from a hook at the back of the house that is attached to the wall fully 15 feet into the air. They have to use a system of pulleys through the bedroom window to retrieve their smalls when the wind has done its stuff.

The result was that with very little effort you could admire the colour of everyone's washing from numbers 1 to 17 down one side of the street, and by swivelling your head slightly you could compare them with numbers 2 to 18 across the way.

I suppose I should at least be grateful to Mrs T for not tying a line to the front of the house and stringing out my smalls down the drive for all the world to see. As it is, only the chickens and the duck get a glimpse of my undergarments, and they seem relatively unimpressed.

As if it were not enough to have given in to the presence of the wretched thing, this morning, while writing in my little upstairs room that looks out over the orchard, I chanced to see the chickens and the duck ambling among the green and leafy scene. The buttercups and daisies were flaunting their flowers in the sun, where the lady of the house flaunts her washing. The sky was the colour of forget-me-nots, and the clouds the colour of my best shirt after Mrs T's ministrations.

Just for a moment I thought to myself what a wonderful scene it made, crisp white sheets fluttering in the breeze. Sort of pastoral. Artisan-like. A real honest-to-goodness country garden. And I felt rather guilty about making all that fuss.

This is why I think that at last I must be losing it. What has happened to my critical faculties? Why am I now prepared to tolerate this linen-draped concoction that once drove me into an apoplectic rage?

Perhaps I like the quiet life too much. But at least I haven't yet felt the need to use a rotary washing line as the centrepiece of a circular garden. No. I'm not that far gone yet. But there is something of HE Bates's Larkins about the view from my window these days. Sort of romantic.

Yup. Worryingly accommodating I'd say. It can't be long before I start to take a shine to gladioli. Now that would be worrying.

2003

There's Chaos in My Order

This tidiness thing is definitely a problem. I always rail at people who go out on a Sunday afternoon to tidy their gardens. I mean, a garden is not a sock drawer. Gardens are not there to be tidied. They are living, breathing, bountiful, billowing organisms and not prim, tight-lipped, inorganic, plant containers.

And yet I do have a little bit of a thing about tidiness in the house, in my study and in the potting shed. My motto is "Don't put it down, put it away." Not that my daughters seem to have cottoned on. But I won't go on about that. It will come back to haunt me if I do.

The trouble is that sometimes it's difficult to stop my household tidiness spilling over into the garden. On occasions it's a good thing. Take weeding, for instance. If I'm sitting down on a garden bench and I see a weed in the middle of the path in front of me, I have to get up and pull it out before I can continue to sit and relax. There is nothing wrong with that, it's what gardening is all about.

But then there are garden ornaments, pots and suchlike. I can take hours positioning them. Well, not hours, but certainly minutes into double figures. Not only do they have to be put in precisely the right spot, but they also have to be spun around until they are at the right angle. You might have thought that a pot, once placed, is very much like another pot placed, but oh dear no. My parks department foreman drilled into me during my apprenticeship "every plant has a front and a back," which is why I can spin a circular container round and know instinctively when its front side is in full view.

If you understand me so far you will be of similar temperament, for which I am grateful. If you don't understand me there is a chance that you will want me committed. But think about it. The plant's front is probably the side that has had the most light, so the shoots are all turning in that direction and the plant looks better from that side. Logical really, isn't it?

What I am concerned about is that my tidy mind should not turn me into one of those gardeners who uses a ruler to plant out their summer bedding. You know the sort: every salvia is precisely nine inches from its neighbour. Every French marigold is exactly six inches from the next one and a line is run along the soil to make sure that they are in ranks as straight as a die.

I'm not joking; I've seen people do it. In a way, this modern fetish for reproducing formal 17th-century parterres is a sort of up-market variation on the regimental bedding scheme. Just watch someone with a potager filled with a row of neat lettuces and tell me if you ever see them pick and eat one.

You've seen photographs of them everywhere, haven't you, those succulent rows of uniform crops dripping with dew? Every lettuce is at the same stage of maturity and not one of them is picked. They don't actually eat them, you know. They are much too frightened of spoiling the symmetry. As soon as one vegetable is harvested, the lot must come up to make the layout neat again. The tidy vegetable plot is the ultimate in sterile gardening.

I think I've found a way around the tidiness obsession in my own garden. I allow myself really strong lines, such as pathways, lawns and low hedges, but between these lines I let the plants go berserk. They can be as rampant and fulsome as they like, provided they don't overstep the mark and fall over the path. If they do, I'm down on them like a ton of shears. Snip. Gone.

But over the years, the gardens I have really enjoyed visiting are those that are not tidy at all, but where the plants grow rampantly and in rich profusion. I love old cottage gardens where tumbling perennials sprawl under lopsided apple trees that are a stranger to the pruning saw. I love kitchen gardens where the wilting leaves of harvested lettuces litter the compost heap, and I am happy to see gaps where the crops have been picked, because then I know it is a proper, working vegetable garden.

Perhaps I am not such a bad case after all. I like daisies in lawns and old man's beard in my hedges. I love flowers that self-seed themselves and roses that scramble through old fruit trees, and I don't think there is any likelihood of me getting like someone I once knew who went out on a Sunday afternoon to do the garden. He stepped out of the front door armed only with a stiff broom. Ten minutes later he came back, his gardening finished. He had, he said, swept the square of concrete free of leaves and the front garden was tidy again. I still can't think about it without a shudder.

1999

The Listed Loo

When I was small, a visit to Grandma Titch, my father's mother, was viewed with some trepidation, not least because she could be a bit fierce. She mellowed in later years to become a lovely little old lady, but having three children and being widowed relatively early on had made her understandably tough during my early years. But it wasn't just Grandma's severity that made a visit to Dean Street a bit of an ordeal – it was her sanitary arrangements. You see, Grandma had an outside lavatory.

In summer, this presented no hardship. It was barely 10 feet from the back door – just half a dozen steps away – but in winter, with the wind whistling and the sleet stinging your face, it was not a journey to relish. Nor was the distempered interior, the icy-cold wooden seat or the Izal paper on a roll on the back of the door.

But I go into too much detail. The nub of the matter is that an outside loo is generally not something to be proud of. And yet, when we moved house four years ago, we found ourselves in possession of one. The sanitary fittings had long gone, but the little hipped-roof brick building, measuring just six by five, stands under the old yew tree right in the middle of the garden.

There is no question of getting rid of this chamber of secrets. It is Grade II listed. How about that then? A listed loo! So if it couldn't be got rid of (and, anyway, I think it's rather cute), I had to decide what to do with it. We stored the garden chairs in it for a while, but it was too much faffing around to extricate them from the confined space, so it sat empty and the spiders took over.

And then, I had a touch of inspiration. A few years ago, I'd visited Helen Dillon's garden in Dublin and been blown away by its wonderful ebullience and classic style. While I was there, I had to use her inside loo (stick with me, there is a reason why I am telling you this). I opened the door to be confronted with the most magnificent shell grotto I have ever seen. Well, that was it. My loo would become a shell grotto.

I broke the news to my family, who immediately considered a sectioning order, but I managed to convince them of the beauty of such a garden feature and knew my idea had been accepted when my birthday present arrived. It was a big box of shells.

Armed with several large bucketfuls of industrial-strength tile fixative, I am now converting the in-convenience into a magical grotto that will become my garden's folly. I haven't got very far yet – just one section of the far wall has been completed – but on dreary or wet days when I want a break from the earth, I go into the privy and put up a few ormers or cockles or mussels. And I have to tell you that it's going to look a treat, even if it will not quite achieve the grandeur of Helen Dillon's Louis XV's version.

But, as is always the case, one idea led to another, and the prospect of having another folly has taken hold of my imagination. Behind the back of the barn is my area of meadow, planted up with crab apples and flowering cherries. It's not massive in estate terms – only about an acre – but there is a long crab-apple-lined ride with a seat at the end. Just a plain wooden bench. It's very nice to sit on, but it's not of any great consequence. If I were to build a small folly there, I would have a focal point *par excellence*. Maybe a miniature castle with a turret and a moat. Or perhaps a pagoda – a diminutive version of Kew's. Or a pyramid or an aviary or a ... you see how one's imagination can run away with one.

And yet, I bemoan the demise of the folly – the handsome architectural statement put up (usually by the landed gentry, it has to be admitted) partly for fun and partly to show the owner's superiority. Modern building regulations are in part responsible for their decline in numbers, but are we so lacking in a sense of humour and so laden with the 'if we can't have one, why should they?' mentality that we're happy to see follies banished from the face of the earth?

The interior and garden designer David Hicks got round the planning problem rather neatly when his local council refused to let him build a stone pyramid in the corner of one of his fields. Instead, he built a pyramid out of marine ply and towed it to the perfect spot on a trailer. You could not see the trailer from his house because it was masked by long grass and so he found the perfect – albeit merely temporary – solution.

So while I am patting my shells into position on the walls of the privy (sorry, grotto), I shall be musing on the form that my new folly will take and wondering if I will manage to convince the local council (and my neighbours) that it adds to the aesthetic appeal of our little bit of countryside.

Do you think I'll succeed?

2007

You Are What You Dig

They say that people grow to look like their dogs, and the other way round. I have a theory that some gardeners grow to look like their soil. No, before you sneer, let me explain. If you spend forty years gardening on the same patch of earth it is bound to have some kind of physical effect on you, and I don't just mean backache.

Take gardeners who have the pleasant task of forking through sand every week of the year. It's light and easy to work, even after a thunderstorm. Nothing there to get a gardener down. Gardeners with sandy soil are light and easy. Mind you, sandy soil can't hold on to nutrients and is rather thin. As a result it produces vegetables which are small and not mightily nourishing. It therefore stands to reason that gardeners with sandy soil are also likely to be thin and undernourished. Only if they go against the grain and ladle on masses of manure will they begin to grow fat, but then they've changed the nature of their soil and so their nature will change too.

You see it's all common sense really. Gardeners with heavy clay soil are heavy for the same reason. Their earth is impossible to dig in wet weather and hard as rock when it's dry. When it does hit that happy medium where cultivation is possible it takes real meat to shift a single spadeful. Ergo, gardeners with clay soil are beefy. They have to be.

What happens, you may ask, when a thin and weedy gardener with sandy soil moves to an area of clay soil? You just watch and see. Over the years the slight frame will become more muscular, the fatter produce that is grown will have an effect on the waistline, and before you can say "manure" that once slight gardener will be a horticultural Chippendale.

There are, of course, a lot of happy, average people with gardens. That is quite simply because they are digging their way through happy, average loam. Nothing strange about that. But you will certainly notice a difference between gardeners on acid soil and those on chalk.

Now far be it from me to cast aspersions, but I have noticed that rhododendron growers of my acquaintance do tend to be a bit sour. Maybe it's because I garden on chalk, but I have noticed that gardeners with chalk soil can soothe every situation. They are the Milk of Magnesia of the gardening world: conscious of their difference from those of a more acid nature.

There is only one group of gardeners I would have no truck with at all. Those on stony soil. Stones in the garden, like those in the kidney, the shoe, the gall or the glasshouse, lead to nothing but trouble and discomfort. Don't say I didn't warn you.

1993

Back to the Nursery

You've got to be a bit of a dreamer to get the most out of your garden, well, that's what I think. I probably dream more than most, but then I've had a lot of practice. When I started as a child, I dreamed of the flowers that would emerge from the sprinkled contents of a packet of seeds. Alyssum was one of the first things I sowed, and what I had not understood at all was the relative scale of the plants. I thought that they would all be as big as hydrangeas. Go on, take a look at an alyssum plant and magnify it to the power of a hundred. It's a hydrangea.

But I weathered the disappointment and carried on. The flowers, though small, had a far better fragrance than the hydrangeas that grew in the corner of the garden.

Then I bought some young dahlia plants and dreamed about the masses of flowers I would cut in late summer. I bought my plants in early May. In Yorkshire, you don't put dahlias out until the end of May or early June, and so they stood in the hall on a shelf above the night storage heater. They did get a bit leggy, but they did not let me down come August and September. I can still remember a brand-new variety called 'Frolic', a pink cactus flushed with creamy yellow. The raiser told me I would be the first person to grow it. Happy memories.

But do the dreams fade as you grow older? I don't think so. They help to keep gardening fresh. Many people dream of retiring and owning a second-hand bookshop. I guess that's because it's a calming sort of job, Radio 3 playing in the background, erudite conversationalists popping in for the odd volume. I think I'd love it for a week. Then I'd probably climb the shelves out of boredom.

No. My real dream is the gardener's alternative to the bookshop, the little nursery. I can see it quite clearly in my mind's eye. It's not too large, has wonderful alluvial soil and is by a river, one that doesn't flood.

It's not an original dream, all gardeners cherish it at one time or another. There is the appeal of self-sufficiency, of specialising in the plants you love and not growing the ones you hate. I'd like one or two old greenhouses with brass knobs, filled with potted treasures and the smell of damp earth, and a potting shed with racks of clay flowerpots. And an old till.

What do you mean it's not realistic? Isn't that the whole point of dreams? And yet, some gardeners do pursue this dream and spend their lives growing certain kinds of plants to the exclusion of all others in little nurseries up and down the land. If you talk to them, they are bound to tell you how rotten it is in winter when your fingers freeze off, and how they just about manage to make a living, but the BMW will have to remain, for them, a dream. And all these EU rules and regulations, such a pain.

And yet I suspect, if you speak to them in spring and summer and ask them to swap jobs, they would tell you where to get off. They do the job because they are devoted to it, and because they understand the pleasures to be had from doing things on a small scale and doing them well.

All of which makes me want to seek out these people and buy their plants. I want to encourage the little man who knows all the answers to growing alpines or orchids or lilies.

Oh, I don't want to stamp out the gardening superstore any more than I want to rid the country of our supermarkets; they both have their parts to play. But, as gardeners, we should encourage those who grow plants for plants' sake and pursue their dreams on our behalf.

Lots of specialist nurseries sell their plants by mail-order and, until you've received a parcel through the post, packed perfectly so that all the inmates arrive at their new garden in tip-top condition, you've not lived. Again, it's a part of the dream, you sit down with the catalogue, see the plants in your mind's eye, work out your design and then make out your order. A border can arrive on your doorstep within days, wrapped up in brown paper. Yes; it will take a year or two to mature, but that's all part of the process.

So if one day, a few years hence, you find yourself walking along the riverbank, and you look over a stone wall and see a little nursery where an old man is hoeing between rows of plants, and you think he looks familiar but you are not sure why, take a closer look. He is older now, and greyer, but he's still identifiable as the guy who used to do it on the telly.

You never know. I might, one day, decide to make that dream come true. In the meantime, I shall keep patronising those who are already doing so, with just the faintest hint of wistfulness.

2001

JULY

Water Quandary

Don't speak to me. I'm in a state of shock. I should be used to it by now. It always happens at this time of year. Some people have a drink problem; I have a lack of drink problem. It's the water – apparently, when I want it, I can't have it.

Each year, in summer, I vent the old spleen at the water board, which makes my life a mite tricky as my secretary is married to a water board executive. She gets very tight-lipped if I so much as bring a bottle of Perrier into the house, and if you leave a tap running she is liable to behave extremely unreasonably.

This puts me in a quandary. As well as needing water for all the usual gardening reasons – washing scale insects off my orange trees, squirting greenfly from my roses and occasionally moistening compost and lawn when there's not a sprinkler ban in force – this year I want to make a lake. Well, actually it's a large pond. A very large pond. When does a pond become a lake? When there's a hosepipe ban.

I rang up the water board. I don't think I spoke to my secretary's husband, but then I couldn't be sure. "How many gallons will it hold?" asked the chap. "Quite a few," I hazarded. "You can fill it up with a hosepipe from your tap provided you hold it and don't leave it unattended," he said. I asked him if he felt it was reasonable to expect me to stand in the middle of a field holding a hosepipe for three or four days.

"Oh, it's that big, is it?" came the reply. "You'd better write in." I'm sure Capability Brown never had to stand holding a hose while the lakes on his grandest commissions filled up. The man at the water board explained that such profligate use of water would have to be metered.

"Can I buy it by the tanker load?" I enquired. "Yes, but we don't sell it that way; you'll have to buy it from someone else." He didn't tell me who. But presumably the people I'd buy it off will already have bought it from the water board and will then charge me even more.

I heard a man on the local news the other night saying that the problem was that some parts of the country had lots of water but that it was too costly to put in pipelines to ship this to the deprived parts of the country because water was such a cheap commodity. Not by the time it gets to me, mate.

So should you have any ideas as to how, monsoons being rare in my neck of the woods, a chap can fill a large hole in the ground with water (short of buying a million crates of Buxton Spring and having a lake that is truly sparkling) I'd be grateful. Failing that, the family will have to take it in turns to hold the hosepipe. I may be gone sometime ...

1991

Behind the Names

Dorothy Parker once wrote, "This is not a book to be tossed aside lightly; it should be thrown with great force." Now that's what I call a book review; honest to a fault, clear and uncompromising. But I've just put down a book that most definitely does not fall into that category: *How It All Began in the Garden* by Maurice Baren.

This is not, as you might think, a treatise on Adam and Eve but a collection of stories that reveals the true identities of folk behind the names that are now so familiar to gardeners. It will tell you who Ena Harkness was, it names the Lawson behind Lawson cypress, and spills the beans that *Viola* 'Jackanapes' was named after Gertrude Jekyll's pet monkey.

Now Maurice Baren is an old mate of mine. We were apprentices in the Parks Department nursery at Ilkley in Yorkshire. His book makes a great read, but I did notice that there are a few plant names whose backgrounds Maurice has left untouched, so perhaps I can furnish you with the stories behind a couple of them.

My research, as regular readers of this page will know, is invariably long and arduous, turning up little-known facts that others may have overlooked in their perusal of the local lending library. My own eclectic collection of volumes has served me well over the years and on this occasion they have, once again, yielded some fascinating, and hitherto obscure, facts.

For instance, it is generally assumed that the apple that fell on Isaac Newton's head was of the variety 'Newton Wonder'. A not unreasonable assumption to those of an obvious turn of mind. Alas, this variety was not raised until a century after Newton's death. In fact, my research has revealed that the apple variety was no other than good old 'Norfolk Beefing'. At the time of the discovery of gravity (for we must remember that it was not Isaac who invented it, he just suffered from it), Mr Newton was holidaying in Cromer. It was not, by all accounts, a happy time. Isaac was a lover of hilly countryside and Norfolk is very flat.

Seeking solace, Isaac took his copy of a first edition Mills & Boon to while away the hours under an old apple tree. It was at the point when the dusky hero was about to rip the bodice from the fair-skinned heroine, that the one fruit on the tree decided that it was time to propagate the species. It fell, with some considerable force, not onto Isaac's head, as is often reported, but onto the open book.

It had not been a good summer. Wet weather had exacerbated the development of brown rot in apples. The apple that fell was rotten, rendering the page of the book totally illegible.

For Isaac Newton it was the last straw and he strode indoors to complain to his mother; a delicate lady without whom he could not travel. But by this time she had had enough. "Stop beefing about Norfolk and go and do something useful about gravity," she said. And so he did. And now 'Norfolk Beefing' reminds us of his holiday that may have been tiresome at the time, but went on to make his name.

I have space to clear up just one last anomaly in the naming stakes: that of the rose 'Iceberg'. The name now commemorates a white variety, but originally it was given to one that was dark crimson. The famous rose breeder, Cyril van der

Pumpenhausen, was deeply proud of his latest success: a full-centred, velvety rose with a pleasant scent. He cut a bunch and took them with him on a celebratory world cruise. On deciding to ask the captain of the ship to name the rose, he strode up to the bridge with an armful to present to the master of the vessel.

Inhaling deeply, the captain quite forgot where he was and found himself transported by the scent of the roses. So much so that he let go of the ship's wheel.

"And vot vould you like me to call ze rose?" asked Cyril. At which point the captain came back to earth and remember that he had not looked at the view from the bridge for some time. He gazed through the glass, momentarily froze, and then uttered the strangulated cry, "Iceberg!".

Alas, too late, Cyril, his roses, the captain and most of the passengers were lost. The rose was named, and then quickly forgotten, on the *Titanic*. Perhaps Maurice will include the story in his next book. It is not, after all, a tale to be tossed aside lightly.

1994

A British Obsession

When I'm travelling by train, I love to look at back gardens. There's a great sense of peeping into people's private worlds. Yes, I know it's a bit of a nerve, but then they knew the railway was there when they bought the houses so I don't see why I should feel too bad.

The feelings each garden generates in me will be quite different. There will be sadness at a plot that has become a dumping ground for scrap metal, old kitchen cupboards and a rusty motorbike, the wistful romanticism fostered by a patch that has not been touched for years and is awash with brambles and white-flowered convolvulus, and the pangs of guilt at the sight of decking and a blue fence.

But there will be pleasurable moments, too: a bright border, a handsome tree, a well-tended lawn. All will set me thinking about that British obsession that is unique to our gardens: tidiness.

Oh, we do love to be tidy. A friend's father once showed me his only gardening tool. It was a soft broom. He used it to sweep the concrete every Saturday. There were no flower-beds in his garden, and no lawn. They would have allowed nature to flex her muscles, and when nature flexes her muscles, gardeners get nervous.

Now, although this chap was an extreme case, there is a degree of obsessive tidiness in all of us. It is a natural trait. We know what we are like, compared with the rest of the world. And we know what they are like too. The Italians are excitable. The Americans are over-emotional. The French are arrogant, and the British are anal.

Oh, you can wrap it up however you like, but it's a general truth. We love to worry, and tidiness, especially in the garden, is a manifestation of that. The trouble is that it is completely unnatural. Nature is never tidy. Anything but. Take autumn. What does she do? She scatters leaves all over the place and doesn't sweep them up. That means the gardener has to get out the barrow and the broom and tidy them away.

If only he'd waited a while, thinks Mother Nature. You see, what she would have done is to have enlisted the help of the wind to blow them into all corners of the garden, against walls and fences. Here they would have rotted down and been returned to the soil as enrichment, in the meantime providing places of hibernation for tiny critters.

When nature sees grass growing she sends in a cow or a sheep to eat the grass and keep it mown, then it recycles the clippings in its stomach and returns them to the land as manure. Neat eh? And what does the gardener do? Takes off the clippings and puts them in a black bin liner, which is then hidden among the other stuff in the wheely bin in the hope that the waste-disposal operative won't notice. And the grass goes hungry.

Then there are the pests. A naturalist might think creepy-crawlies have as much right to be there as we do, but the gardener does not see it that way at all. We love to see our lawn edges clipped neatly so that there is not a blade out of place, and yet we cannot appreciate the skill of the leafcutter bee on our roses. Shame.

And we worry about pruning. How we worry about pruning. "Norman! That tree's getting too big." That tree has probably dared to approach Norman's height and that will make him nervous. Time to take out the saw and the loppers and show it who's boss.

You see, you have to prune things in a garden in order to get them to flower well and to keep them, you guessed it, neat. No matter that nature doesn't prune. Nature, after all, has more space. Ah, but wouldn't it just make more sense to choose plants that would be in scale with our gardens, rather than having to be butchered to fit? No, too much research needed at the outset. Easier to buy something you like the look of and bully it into submission. Is all this sounding a tad grumpy? I don't mean it to be. It's just that the perversity of gardeners, and I include myself, can be counterproductive.

So what's the answer? Perhaps a slightly more relaxed attitude to our gardens: not in the rusty motorbike and brambles league, but in the willingness to let plants romp and scramble without being corseted, sprayed and butchered.

I mean, when was the last time you wandered along a British hedgerow in summer and said to yourself, "Look at the mildew on that cow parsley, and most of those buttercups need digging up and dividing"? Of course you didn't. You just enjoyed it for what it was: a relaxed planting of lovely things all jumbled together and having a wonderful time growing. It's exhilarating to look at, isn't it? Far more exhilarating than a bed of petunias planted out with military precision, or a rose bed carpeted with weed-free grey earth.

So, next time you reach for the broom, the shears or the sprayer, just pause for a moment and ask yourself, "Do I really need to?" You never know. Left to her own devices Mother Nature might just produce something wonderful.

2003

Predictably Unpredictable

When two Englishmen meet the first thing they talk about is the weather, remarked Dr Johnson in the 18th century. And we still do, but then it's not really surprising, as we always have so much of it to talk about. There would be no point in wittering on about it in the Sahara. "It's a nice day for this time of year," would be inappropriate among the sand dunes and Mrs Eskimo could be forgiven for filing for divorce if her husband on looking out of the window each morning said, "It's snowy outside, Mabel." It's the total unpredictability of our weather that makes it such a talking point.

I mean, take the other day. I was out walking the dogs at eight in the morning on the most blissful, still, sunny day. I actually flung my arms out wide, à la Julie Andrews in *The Sound of Music*, and told them both that it was a wonderful morning. They didn't take any notice. And then I felt rather stupid.

I felt even more stupid the following day when, at the same hour, I battled through the drizzle in my waxed jacket and flat hat as the fine rain stung my cheeks. But British gardeners are somewhat used to the vicissitudes of meteorology and we wouldn't have things any other way.

I think the relative unpredictability of the weather is actually rather reassuring. If you worry about genetic engineering and the hand of Big Brother, isn't it rather nice to know that he can't do much about the weather except put up an umbrella or don sunglasses?

Mind you, the Russians did recently try to put more sunshine into their long, dark arctic winters by sending a massive mirror into orbit to reflect the sun's rays. But it went wrong. They couldn't get it to open or something. And I'm glad as I'm not a control freak. When it comes to the weather, you simply get what you're given. Or you move away.

That said, there are some types of weather that really get my back up. Wind, for instance. It makes me irritable. But then wind, whether inside or out, has that effect on most people. And on cats. What is it about wind and the feline? Mine go mad when there's a strong breeze. They have a crazy look in their eyes and suddenly run off in an unexpected direction and up a tree. Then they'll try to climb across the sky upside down. And fall.

It's hard for a gardener to think of something good to say about wind. It usually brings destruction, especially when it lashes young leaves early in the year. I know that it blows the old ones down in autumn, but it also blows them where they aren't wanted, usually all over the lawn and the drive.

And don't believe those people who say that wind blows pests away. While yours are blowing into someone else's garden, someone else's are blowing into yours. So it doesn't so much get rid of them as pass them around.

Sunshine we all like as it charges up our batteries. We've also reached the stage where most of us would like to be reminded what a drought is like. Last summer? Don't make me laugh. If the water board bans hosepipes this year there will be a few gardeners who will want them committed.

Of course, being a son of the soil, I am expected to be able to predict the weather in advance. A shepherd friend and I were talking one spring a few years ago. "Have you any feelings about the summer?" I asked. "Yes," he said. "I reckon it's going to be a scorcher."

I thought just the same. What happened? It poured from June to September. However, I still have sympathy for weather forecasters, although I feel a sneaking satisfaction when they get it wrong. Not because it shows any sort of failing on their part. Not at all. They have all the best technology, the most up-to-date computers and the most sophisticated prediction techniques, but no one can predict the unpredictable and the weather is, more than anything else, capricious.

That's why you won't hear that I'm moving to some tropical paradise, where it rains at noon every day for an hour and then the sun comes out. It would drive me mad. I suppose I like being gloomy when it rains, and I'm happy to complain that I can't go up the garden without making a squelching sound. And all because one morning at eight o'clock, when it's clear and sunny, I can't help feeling like a million dollars.

In California, of course, the sun shines all the time, but look at them on *Baywatch*. They are as miserable as sin. The problem? Too much sunshine. What they need is a few days of dull skies and torrential rain so that they could put away their tiny red swimsuits and crouch in their beach huts with an anorak and a Primus stove. Every Brit knows that you can't beat a good bit of complaining about the weather to cheer yourself up.

1999

On the Origin of Faeces

The other day, as I was digging in a luscious helping of good old farmyard manure, it struck me how unadventurous we are with fertiliser. A century ago gardeners were much more outlandish in the enrichment they used. But today's gardeners seem to have far fewer effluents to hand.

You only have to look down at the local garden centre. There is spent mushroom compost, with its lumps of chalk, and concentrated manure. One bag must contain the waste products of goodness knows how many cows. Then there's spent hops and composted bark. But none of them possesses that earthy fragrance that tells you what goes in must come out.

At least with a trailer-load of farmyard manure you know what you are getting. Well, actually, perhaps you don't. I mean, it all depends on what's available in the farmyard. Do the farmers just mean horses and cows, or are there free-range chickens and geese as well. And what about the pigs?

How many people can still lay their hands on pig manure? Well, maybe not their hands, but their spades. Do pigs do it in one place, or have you to run after them with shovel? I'm sorry to be indelicate, especially if you are about to dine, but a chap needs to know.

I think the farmyard manure I was gleefully spading into my soil was mainly cow manure. It came from Mr Perkins down the road and he hasn't got horses, just a few cows that he gives shelter to and I guess that the manure was the sweepings from out of the byre.

But what happens if you live in the town? Do you have to buy that concentrated stuff when half the beauty of manure is its bulk? As well as being rich in nutrients, you see, manure has the ability to improve soil structure, to open it up and give it a bit of body. You can feel the goodness and you know the nutrients are there because you've read it somewhere.

Now when I was a nipper and first took to this gardening lark, we had a man who came with a lorry from Halifax selling the Corporation's waste products in bright yellow sacks. The waste products had been treated, you understand, but they were a kind of fibrous, shoddy-based manure that was a really good soil improver.

And the smell! Ah, the richness of it! That kind of acrid fertiliser smell that just shouts out nutrients. The name of this fertiliser from Halifax is one I shall never forget. It was called Organifax. Nifty eh? I wonder if it still exists? It did my dahlias a power of good.

Another one was produced in Dagenham, according to a London friend of mine. It was called Dagfert. Not quite the same ring to it as Organifax. Do any of the local government organisations still produce their own soil enrichment? I'd like to know, if only to add a new name to my brief list of two.

What I can vouch for is the efficacy of chicken manure. The five hens I keep have a coop inside their run which is carpeted with straw. Once littered by their droppings, it makes a great accelerator for the compost heap.

Chicken manure is probably the only kind of avian enrichment available to today's gardeners. Whatever happened to canary guano? I have a wondrous advertisement poster that shows a Hitchcockian flock of bright yellow canaries descending from a mountain. "The Chemical Union Ltd, Ipswich", it reads. "Canary Guano, the best in the world, for greenhouse and garden". It doesn't say where it came from or how many canaries it took to produce it, but guano seems to have gone out of fashion, if not out of existence.

Mind you, there are one or two fertilisers I am not sorry to see the back of. Digested sewage sludge never sounded to me like something I wanted to spread on my salad crops.

I suppose there are a few organic consolations left to the gardener: dried blood, steamed bone flour, hoof and horn, and fishmeal. All of them smell as if they should be doing plants a power of good, which is more than you can say for some of the inert and lifeless grey fertiliser granules you get now.

Perhaps that, after all, is the essence of manuring. Rather like medicine which is supposed to do you more good the worse it tastes, manure is better the worse it smells. After all, the best-flavoured tomatoes I ever tasted were fed on liquid manure from a fetid tank in which a sack of sheep manure was suspended. Now I really have put you off your tea. Cheese and tomato sandwich anyone?

1995

You Can't Please Everyone

Growing old disgracefully has always struck me as a laudable aim. I say that, and yet when it comes to the crunch I'll probably chicken out. But I know that geriatric rebellion is a popular concept. Jenny Joseph's poem about ageing got to number 22 in a survey carried out a couple of years ago to discover the nation's favourite poems. You know the one I'm referring to, all about wearing purple clothes, learning to spit and eating three whole pounds of sausages in one go. I happen to think it's a cracking poem and an inspiration to us all. But I do worry that I'll fall short of its aims and remain polite and considerate to the bitter end.

There is no doubt that this course of action is a big mistake. It makes a rod for your own back. I mean, it stands to reason that if you continue to say yes to people, they will continue to ask you to do things. It would be far better to say no at the outset, be thought a grumpy old sod and live a quiet, untroubled life. Wouldn't it?

When I've sent off 11 signed books to charity auctions in one week, provided seven recipes for charity cook books and mailed 23 signed photographs, how great is the temptation to succumb to one of George Bernard Shaw's little quirks and have some postcards printed with the words, "Alan Titchmarsh regrets that he is unable to agree to your request." Neat that. Succinct. But also a bit rude and ungrateful. But then, you see, George Bernard Shaw was older than I am. And wiser.

He would have had just the right words to respond to a letter I received this week from a garden centre manager complaining that I had written a piece on hardy annuals in which I'd said that they represented a much cheaper way of growing summer flowers than buying bedding plants at a garden centre. "The garden centre industry is not enjoying a good time at the moment, mainly because of the weather. A few positive messages would help, rather than negative ones." Well, that put me in my place.

I wrote back, politely, explaining that my position as a television gardener and writer was a difficult one because, while I felt the need to support the industry, I also wanted to show people how to become good gardeners, which often means growing plants themselves.

I did point out that his complaint was akin to that of a restaurant owner criticising a cookery programme. I wonder if Jamie Oliver gets letters telling him off for showing viewers how to make their own soufflés and the like and, in doing so, endangering the very livelihood of Marco Pierre White, Raymond

Blanc and Gordon Ramsay? Somehow I expect that these guys take the broader view.

At least the garden centre owner made his criticism by post. I was in the supermarket the other day with Mrs T when, half-way down the cold meats aisle, we were rammed by a lady shopper. Oh, it was no accident. She positioned her trolley with all the skill of Michael Schumacher on the starting grid. Then she smiled. "You don't remember me do you?" I had to confess that I did not. "I wrote to you two years ago," she said.

"Did you get a reply?" I asked.

"No."

"Oh. Sorry. I do try to reply to all my letters, there are several hundred every week, so . . ."

"And I wrote a poem." She proceeded to recite it. In the middle of the cold meats. I pulled in so other shoppers, even more bewildered than me, could overtake. It was nothing like Jenny Joseph's masterpiece, but began "Oh Mr Titchmarsh, what shall I do? I wanted a lovely garden but . . . di-do-di-do-di-do." I don't recall the rest. But I did listen. For several minutes. "And I'm only up the road" was her final rejoinder.

At the end of her peroration the lady turned to my wife and said, "I suppose you get fed up with all this, don't you?" To her enduring credit, my wife smiled a smile that was as sunny and serene as that of any angel and said . . . absolutely nothing. The lady, crushed by kindness, bowed her head and pushed her trolley on towards wet fish.

That, I think, will be my modus operandi in future. I shall not become curmudgeonly after the fashion of George Bernard Shaw; I shall not wear purple and learn to spit. No. I shall learn serenity in the face of churlishness and calmness in the grip of criticism and, as a result, I shall live longer, smile more broadly and be thought of as a lovely man by all and sundry.

But when I get home I will close all the windows and scream loudly. It's probably better that way.

2001

The Grand Design

You know, sometimes I think we get too precious when it comes to designing our gardens. We draw up plans (well, we're *told* to draw up plans), we devise colour schemes, we include focal points, minimalist water features and viewpoints, and all too often we forget the innate charm of the plants themselves, and the happy accidents that can happen with them.

Now, I wouldn't like you to think that I'm being holier than thou about this. I am as guilty as the next man of planning my garden to death. Then I'll call in at a friend's garden and discover a corner where the old greenhouse meets an ancient brick wall. A pile of moss-covered clay flowerpots are slithering into a corner, there is a stray branch of honeysuckle flowering its hat off, and some forget-me-nots have self-seeded under its bough and . . . well, I wonder why I bother with all that arty-farty stuff.

You've probably encountered corners like this yourself. They happen more by chance than design, and that's how some of my best plant combinations have occurred – not by meticulous planning and observation, but as a result of serendipity.

I noticed one in my garden this spring, which involved the flowers of the hellebore that is rather oddly known as *H. x ericsmithii* (serves Eric right for having such a run-of-the-mill surname – the botanists obviously felt they had to include his Christian name too, to differentiate him from all the other Smiths). Anyway, I have three Erics planted where some self-sown seedlings of that purple cow parsley, 'Ravenswing', are pushing up, and the bronzy-brown of the cow parsley is the perfect complement to the green and pink flowers of the hellebores. It's not just pleasant, it's remarkable.

I have a similar sort of combination in summer involving David Austin's modern English shrub rose 'Eglantyne' (named after Eglantyne Jebb, one of the founders of Save the Children). I've planted her in front of that newish elder *Sambucus* 'Black Lace'. The soft peachy flowers of the rose are thrown into crisp relief against the plum-black feathery foliage of the sambucus. This combination was planned, but I didn't know just how effective it would be – there is a hint of the peach tone buried deep in the colour of the elder, and the one brings out the other.

Of course, from time to time, plants are produced that have the worst colour schemes possible. They are not pleasant, they are not even tolerable, they just give you a sickly feeling in your stomach. I mean, why would anyone want to market *Ceanothus* 'Zanzibar'? Its leaves are green, edged and blotched with acid yellow, and the flowers are powder blue. In no way is this combination of colours pleasing. Gertrude Jekyll will be revolving in her summerhouse in the sky. I can recommend it as an alternative to salt water as an emetic any day.

That little moisture lover *Houttuynia Cordata* 'Chameleon' is equally un-endearing. Its leaves are a combination of green, luminous red and sickly orange – as though an indecisive painter just dabbed his brush into every colour and splashed it on. Never has the term 'riot of colour' been more applicable to one plant than it has to this houttuynia. But it's popular, so clearly some folk just want 'colour' and care not what the combination is.

You could argue that colour combinations are a totally subjective thing, and that if you like a particular plant mixture you should be able to go along with it. I would be the last person to stop you, but then in books of garden design, or interior design, there are examples of schemes that are effective, defined as being in 'good taste'. We might not want to live in them ourselves, but generally speaking we can see that they work.

Clearly there are combinations that all of us regard as being happy. The trick is to use them in your own garden, without it looking like everybody else's, and the fact that there are now over 70,000 different varieties of choice in the RHS *Plant Finder* probably makes that easier than it used to be.

Mind you, most garden centres stock a limited range of plants, so to increase your chance of 'happy accidents' you must be adventurous and try different things, especially from specialist nurseries and seedsmen. It's what keeps gardeners fresh and gardens different. Rather like composing. Given the same notes, it's unlikely two composers would come up with the same tune. But we, like them, must keep pushing the boundaries, and be daring.

So the next time you are planning your garden, by all means get your lines right and your focal points in the right place, but give yourself enough elastic, enough freedom to try things out. A chance to go wrong a bit and then try something else.

The alternative is that you go for the minimalist look – a sea of one particular plant with a stainless steel or granite monolith rising through it. Effective? Yes. Modern? Yes. But if it is the only sort of thing you can find in your garden, it's also a bit of a cop-out. Give me moss-covered flowerpots any day.

2006

AUGUST

Diary Entry

I wish I had been more assiduous about keeping a diary. Alas, my attempts always end in failure, and have done ever since I was small.

As soon as I showed an interest in gardening, the Christmas present list was made easier and, from age 10 or 11, I could bank on a Gardener's Diary finding its way into my stocking. I have one still, dated 1964, my first year at work in the Parks Department nursery, and it is full of such enlightening information as: "My turn on boilers, so I did them."

As a social document, it is of doubtful value, even if it does give an indication of the state of greenhouse heating systems in the early 1960s. The entries, each one outdoing the next for crushing banality, peter out altogether on about 18 January. Two and a half weeks – that seems to have been the approximate going rate for my diary stamina.

Every year, now, I toy with starting a proper diary, recording things that happen in a witty and engaging way, but there is always a reason why I should not.

It's the wrong time of year. Who starts a diary in August? Or, I am invited to some glittering event and think I really ought to keep a record of who was there and what they said. But wouldn't that just put people's backs up? If I'm wittering on about someone famous saying this, and someone else saying that, surely folk will just think, "Oh, hark at him."

I was at a dinner the other day, talking to Michael Palin (you see, that's the sort of thing I mean), and he confessed that he had kept a diary for years – since just before his son was born. It also coincided with the getting together of the *Monty Python* team. I congratulated Michael on the wisdom of embarking on what would clearly become an important cultural document of a critical time in the history of British comedy.

He conceded that this was not his intention. He had given up smoking and needed something to take his mind off it, and a diary was the answer. "I suppose it was a bit anal, really," he said, and added that most of the entries concerned the birth and development of his son, rather than what John Cleese said on a particular day. But doubtless there will be enough of Cleese to make it a good read.

I do have a diary, but it is simply a list of engagements – of filming dates and meetings, holiday dates and nights out. Not much mileage there for the social commentator. My gardening diary is non-existent, although I do, within the working diary, keep a rough sketch of where different plants are when I put them in – the crab apples in the orchard, the row of 30 hostas at the back of the border – as an insurance policy against the day when the labels are lost or spirited away.

The trouble is that to check out what is where, I need to remember the year in which I planted a particular feature. Not always easy, since this would invariably mean wading through a pile of old diaries.

So although I might have failed to meticulously log the intricacies of my daily life, I have decided to keep a gardening logbook, and have now transferred these lists and lumps of information to a single volume, in order to make life easier.

There are plans of borders and maps of beds. Notes of what was purchased where and when. But it's a joyless read. There is no colour, only facts. I suppose it will improve with time – when I'm amazed that I've had a plant for so long, or reminded that I used to have something which has long since faded away.

Alan Bennett bemoaned the dreariness of his own early diaries, saying that they concentrated, in true adolescent fashion, on his feelings, rather than events – his agonies and preoccupations which, with the passage of time, make dull reading. In the case of Alan Bennett, this is hard to believe, but I see what he means.

Diary writing, whether related to the garden or to life in general, is an art in itself. Read the year-round writing of Vita Sackville-West and set them against your own leaden gardening notes. Or maybe you think yours compare well? Take a look at the diarist's diarist, Samuel Pepys, and marvel at the content of his daily life three-hundred-and-odd years ago.

You see, I need to be spurred on. I shall start a diary soon, no matter what the date, and I shall record wittily the events that embroider my days. I will not lean heavily on the heating system of my greenhouse nor on the meetings with celebrities that might turn it into a hard-backed version of *OK!* Magazine. I shall, instead, write engaging copy that will have my readers on the edge of their seats, wondering what happens next.

Well, that will do for now. I've done the "Got up, made tea, fed chickens, sat at laptop" bit, and it's time for the walk around the garden.

Don't hold your breath for a publication date.

2006

Out of Control

Nature is perverse. It's all very well for us gardeners to put up nest boxes and plant wildflowers and have ponds and all that, but we still have no control over wildlife at large and that makes me miffed.

Since 1982 I have had an open-fronted nest box on my garden shed. "This," said the Royal Society for the Protection of Birds "is of the kind preferred by robins and flycatchers."

That nest box remained on the shed, year in, year out, without so much as a twig by way of nesting material. After year four I'd have been grateful for a crow, never mind a robin. Eventually I moved it to the woods in the hope of success there.

I now sit in my study, fully half a mile from the wood, and outside my window what can I see perched on a branch of my ornamental pear tree? A spotted flycatcher. The excitement on first glimpsing it three days ago was matchless. I fetched the family one by one to watch it cavort as it dashed about in the air, snapping at its prey. It then occurred to me that it had appeared the day after I'd moved the nest box. I'm looking at it now. It's a bit too pleased with itself if you ask me. Where is it nesting? Blessed if I know.

It doesn't stop there either. I've made a pond in the garden for wildlife. Where did I find a frog yesterday? In an upturned dustbin lid that's meant to be a birdbath. Pity the poor black-bird hopping over for his morning dip, only to be goosed by a frog from the murky depths. Again, I have large portions of my garden given over to wildflowers. Huge great areas of nettles for small tortoiseshells and peacocks and red admirals to lay their eggs. They're probably using the nettles that grow among the border plants where I don't want them.

I love slow worms, but where do they live? In the compost heap so that I'm afeared of using it lest I cut them in half.

Hedgehogs are welcome to keep down the slugs, but where do they hibernate? In the bonfire. I have the biggest pile of garden refuse you've ever seen, because I'm too scared to light it in case barbecued hedgehog appears on the menu.

I adore deer, but they eat my roses. Come to think of it they eat everything. The rabbits that romp over the paddock to "aahs" from my wife and children nibble the bark off my fruit trees. I keep three golden Labradors but they can't catch them. One of them can't even see them. And to think I once thought of becoming a vet.

Add to all this a plague of greenfly that I'm supposed to rub off with my fingers on account of being keen on conserva-tion, and I'm a bit depressed at the moment. Have any of these green conservationists actually tried controlling all the greenfly in six acres of land by rubbing them between their fingers? Naah. They're out with the sprayer at dead of night or I'm a Dutchman.

1992

The Kindest Cut

Plants, if only they wouldn't grow. You put them in, you water them and they establish themselves, but then the blighters keep on growing, long after you hope they've reached their ultimate height and spread.

It was the architect Sir Frederick Gibberd who said that gardening was the most difficult of all the art forms: not only are you dealing with size, shape and colour, but you are dealing with time in terms of season and years. Plants will grow larger and larger and then go over the hill. The picture is always changing. It's a tricky business.

It's always struck me as rather sad that a plant is at its best just before it starts to die. Look at a mature oak, standing in the middle of the countryside. Majestic and seemingly impregnable. Then, before you know where you are, its branches start to die and it looks like an impression of Landseer's *Monarch of the Glen*, all stag-headed and spiky.

Well, in the countryside that's all very well, but in your garden it's a bit of a problem when a tree or a shrub goes over the hill. It's been happening in my own garden recently. Not with oak trees, thank goodness, but with shrubs that have been growing there for a good 12 years. They've not gone over the hill, so much as over the top. I've noticed that the lawn is smaller, and then discovered that the branches of a horizontal juniper have cast themselves over it for a good six or eight feet.

Now I'm not as hard-hearted as I should be in the garden. Not where mature plants are concerned. Oh, if they are awful to look at I don't feel much compunction about hauling them out, but if they are doing well, too well, it's hard to do a George Washington and fell them to the ground. But I've done it, and the worrying thing is I think I've developed a taste for it.

You see, once you've made the decision, wiped away the tear and struck with an axe, or in my case a neat little folding pruning saw, the garden begins to open up before you. When the first juniper was out I realised that there was quite a lot of garden underneath it. Garden that could support other plants and, after twelve years or so, you can do with every spare inch of space you can get.

So exhilarated did I feel after my onslaught that I was beginning to think that I had developed a real problem. Perhaps my garden would be razed to the ground before I knew where I was and that only low growing cushion plants and alpines would be safe. But then I talked to Nick Brooks, head gardener at Hinton Ampner garden in Hampshire.

Nick assured me that in the garden there, the delightful creation of Ralph Dutton, the 8th and last Lord Sherborne, he has exactly the same problem, on an even larger scale. The garden was planted up from the late 1930s onwards, so you can imagine the size and shape of some of the trees and shrubs it contains.

Shrubs that are listed in catalogues as being of an ultimate height of 8ft and a spread of 10ft are now, 50 years on, at least twice that, and rather dead in the centre. Some of them are being replaced, and some are being carefully and yet drastically pruned back, to reinvest them with their lost vigour.

It does mean that a plant can look a sorry state immediately after such butchery. But, if the pruning is tailored to the needs of the plant in question then it works and the plant, the garden and the gardener are better off as a result.

All of which is of little consolation to my roses. I have a small rose garden that is planted up with old-fashioned shrub roses. A path runs around it and, after about five years, the roses had strayed too far and kept hauling back anyone rash enough to enter the rose garden in a woolly cardy. I decided on drastic action, just to see what would happen. I cut all the roses back to within a few inches of ground level. I know I'll have to forgo the best part of a display for this year, but I'm hopeful that by next year they will be shapely, not too large and full of flower.

This is not a technique I am recommending as yet. I'll let you know what happens as the summer progresses. But it might well alter the way I look at shrub roses in a small garden. It might also alter the way they look at me.

1995

The Specialist

The epigram, "Specialisation leads to extinction," was thrown at me when I was a student at Kew Gardens by the jaunty, white-haired, potting-shed philosopher who was in charge of the cactus houses, a man who could quote Einstein just as readily as he could EA Bowles.

What he meant was that if you concentrated your efforts into one area of horticulture, you could ignore another to its detriment. It is a perfect counter to that other criticism, "Jack of all trades, master of none."

The trouble with presenting *Gardeners' World* on BBC 2 means that being a Jack of all trades, horticulturally speaking, is vital if the whole gamut of gardening is to be covered throughout the series. There is an alternative; I could wheel in an expert whenever I mention a particular plant, but I think that would be tedious if I did it every time some beauty to which one particular society is devoted hit the screen.

Show a chrysanthemum and up pops a chrysanth expert. Talk about blackfly on broad beans and interview a man from the National Vegetable Society. Pot up a few cuttings and have a word with a potter. It's all going too far.

Don't think that I'm trying to do the National Dahlia Society down or take a swipe at the British Gladiolus Society which, along with many other British horticultural societies, is peopled by fascinating experts with whom you would be delighted to share a lunchtime pint. But such societies are also, let us be perfectly honest about this, patronised by one or two members who are, shall we say, a little less than stimulating. I have a morbid fear of being saddled with a bespectacled boffin in a grey anorak with a fake fur collar who can give me chapter and verse on Himalayan rhododendrons at the drop of a yak. Specialisation, in this instance, could lead to the extinction of viewers.

And yet there are times when I get my comeuppance for trying to be an all-rounder. A few weeks ago, I was at a big Yorkshire flower show when a man pushed his face into mine and said, "Them auriculas you 'ad on yer programme ..."

"Yes?" I offered.

"An' that auricula theatre you 'ad 'em in ..." At last, I thought, someone who has enjoyed this unusual wooden shelf arrangement I've built at Barleywood to show off my pot-grown auriculas and wants to build one in their own garden.

"Wasn't on for no time at all and we stayed in especially to watch it. Right disappointment."

I tried my best to explain that this is the problem with gardening on television. It is a battle with time and that there is so much to be fitted into a half hour programme that the balance sometimes makes one or two items shorter than we would ideally like. That we are aware of this fact and that we really shouldn't try to cram too much ...

"And yer plants were rubbish. If yer wants ter see some decent auriculas, go an' look at our stand over there." In the distance, I could see the black draperies that showed off serried ranks of auriculas, their flowers smothered in white powder and each one as symmetrically perfect as its neighbour. They were, as you have no doubt guessed, the property of the National Primula and Auricula Society.

Well. I tried to politely counter with excuses as to the reasons why my plants were not quite up to such standards and said that a lot of my plants were not show varieties, but simply some that had been grown from seed and grown in pots for fun. It cut no ice.

And then the old cactus grower's aphorism about specialisation and extinction came into my mind. "What do you grow in your garden?" I enquired. "Auriculas," replied the weighty man, leaning threateningly towards me across the trestle table which seemed to be all that was protecting me from being shaken warmly by the neck. "Anything else?" "Primulas." "Is that all?" I asked; "no vegetables, no roses, no geraniums or border plants or anything else at all?"

"No. Just auriculas and primulas."

"So how would you have felt if mine had been better than yours?" All I had to do then was raise my eyebrows and smile. His anger melted away.

His honour had been maintained, the trestle table no longer groaned under the weight of his bulk and his face broke into a wide grin. "Aye. Well mebbe I'll write ter that programme and ask 'em ter give yer a bit longer next time."

Well, you never know. In this case specialisation might lead to extension. I was just relieved that it had not led to my extinction; he was, after all, an awfully big man.

1997

Bold Is Beautiful

When it comes to paintwork in the garden, it will not have escaped your notice that I am no shrinking violet. I am happy to paint a fence lavender blue, a shed daffodil yellow, or a rendered wall terracotta. Mind you, I've taken a bit of flack for it.

I do know that my love of messing about with different shades comes from my childhood. My grandma's house had brown paintwork, but then in the first 40 years of this century everybody's grandma's house had brown paintwork.

This resulted in our parents painting everything magnolia and my generation rebelling by using every colour in the spectrum, having come through the phase of that fail-safe, white with a hint of peach. Never mind the hint, just give me the peach, or preferably the bright orange. Not that I've been quite that bold in a garden. Yet.

When I worked in the Parks Department of my local council, anything and everything to do with the council was painted cream and green. From the walls in the council offices, to the doors and even the window frames of the council houses, it was all cream and green.

Then I moved to the Royal Botanic Gardens in Kew. The benches in the gardens were either plain wood or dark green, while everybody else's garden furniture was white. The latter meant that it was easy to spot a bench in the twilight if you wanted to, well, you know, get to know your girlfriend a bit better, but white as a colour lacks any kind of conviction. In fact, it's not really a colour at all.

There were classy garden designers who scorned the use of white and went for the outlandish eau de nil, a sort of soft, greeny grey. To me it just looked insipid. The Japanese went too far in the other direction, painting their bridges bright pillar-box red. Except that they don't actually have red pillar-boxes in Japan. Perhaps they describe the colour of our pillar-boxes as bridge red.

It was all very confusing and a little bit dispiriting. Then I discovered Snowshill Manor in the Cotswolds, created by Charles Paget Wade. The windows and doors of his house and all the garden furniture were painted a wonderful shade of blue. It looked absolutely sensational. Plants looked good against it and it worked perfectly with the honeyed Cotswold stone. The whole garden had a zingy brilliance that was still very tasteful.

I went home and started to experiment, coming up with a darker shade of blue that looked great on trellises and timber. I haven't used it everywhere, only on the gazebo I call the teahouse and the trellis behind my decking. But it was a start. Elsewhere I have used other colours. Another gazebo, yes alright, I am a two-gazebo family, has been painted a soft, silver-birch grey, with a roof of a pale green colour that looks similar to aging copper.

In other people's gardens during my many *Ground Force* visits, I have painted a wall behind a pergola in Spalding terracotta, the wall of a house in Wood Green in a rich Moroccan blue, and the fence panels of a garden in Torquay a very fetching shade of lavender.

And still there are those people who prefer their fence panels to be brown, or painted with that hideous foxy orange colour that the manufacturers seem to love. I really can't understand why. Oh, they will tell you that it is the plants that should provide the colour and not the fence. But they clearly have not lived in a tiny garden surrounded by interwoven fencing which, for the first five years of the garden's life, is entirely visible and also dominant.

Well, I'm blowed if I want to live within the confines of a dark brown enclosure. Neither do I want my shed to skulk in dingy livery at the bottom of the garden. Granted, my sheds are painted black, but that is because I'm trying to tuck them into the shadows, which is possible in a large garden. In a smaller one, where the shed is prominent, paint it pale blue or yellow with white eaves and you will have transformed it into a small New England house instead of a site hut.

There may be those who don't notice colour in the garden, or who are afraid to stick their necks out. They can keep dull brown. Me? I'm splashing on the colour and living a much brighter life as a result.

1999

Brief Encounters

How many times have I been asked to recommend a plant that will "look good all the year round"? On the surface of things this seems a perfectly straightforward question. I mean, it stands to reason: the better looking a plant remains throughout the year, the more pleasure it will give you, won't it? Nope. Somehow I don't think so.

What? Has the man gone bonkers? Does he imagine a plant will give more pleasure if it looks uninteresting most of the time? Well, in a funny sort of way, yes I do. All right, I'll explain. Picture an apple tree that is never out of blossom. Wouldn't that be wonderful, to have all those coconut-ice pink and white flowers the whole year round? You think so? Believe me, after three months you wouldn't even notice it.

The apple tree's perfection lies in the fact that its blossom period is brief but spectacular. You wouldn't haul your other half out of the house every day to say "come and look at the apple tree in blossom" if it was commonplace. But to watch those wizened branches, be-wigged with grey-green lichen, gradually burst open their downy buds each April and explode with pink and white petals that last one or two weeks at most: now that is worth hauling half the village out to see.

Then the petals fall and the tree passes through a stage of pale green indifference before the apples start to ripen and stud the branches with red orbs. Then you can again call out your soulmate and point out the rosy harvest with consummate pleasure.

If this all sounds a little over the top, it is simply that I have discovered this year, more than any other, the wonder of flowers and plants in their season. There is a wistfulness that comes over me when a group of flowers that has given so much pleasure gradually fades. For a moment I am engulfed in sadness, then I turn to see the next group of plants fattening their buds. So it is that this year I have lurched, in an almost drunken stupor, from snowdrops to daffodils to tulips, from apple blossom to paeonies to roses, and to border perennials and dahlias. Can you get the same thrill from something that "looks good all the year round?" Of course not.

At the risk of sounding like a boring old fart, I remember the nose-tingling thrill of chrysanthemums that opened in October and November. This signalled to me the start of autumn, and the acrid tang at the Civic Ball meant that the year was drawing to a close. Then they developed this technique of having chrysanthemums in bloom all the year round. They did this by regulating day length. It was wonderful for the floristry trade. They could offer folk chrysanths in bunches or in pots, "pot mums", at any time of the year. No thank you. Who wants to be reminded of autumn in spring? In spring I want daffs and tulips.

Ah, but you can have those in autumn too; we've found out how to fool them into thinking it's spring. But why? Here we have nature in all its infinite variety offering us something fresh every season, and we think it's an improvement to make every week of the year the same. Have I lost the plot or what?

We have, in our local town, two very obliging florists who know perfectly well that if I go in for a bunch of flowers there is no point in trying to sell me chrysanthemums in the spring or carnations at any time of the year. Chrysanths belong in autumn and carnations belong in buttonholes. They are not flowers that should be arranged, and anyway, most have lost their fragrance, which for me is the best part of a carnation.

Of course, you may be thinking that I'm in Mr Grumpy mode and that I ought to be grateful for modern developments that make it possible for me to enjoy whatever flower I choose at any time of year. But then I am still sufficiently a man of nature for this all-powerful control to make me feel slightly uneasy.

When I was a kid, grown-ups blamed bad weather on all those rockets "they" sent into space. Now I'm a grown-up myself, I blame it all on mobile phones. Before these arrived, necessity was the mother of invention. Today, the invention becomes the precursor of necessity, if the advertisers have their way. Do you know you will soon be able to watch a film on your mobile phone? Great development, eh? You'll be able to ruin your eyesight far more quickly than if you were to watch a film on a large screen at the cinema or on the telly at home. Does anyone really want to watch a film on a screen one inch square?

It's your age, Alan. Shut up and get on with it. OK. But I'll tell you this. The day they invent an apple tree that blooms the whole year round, or try to palm me off with a Christmas cactus in July, is the day I'm outta here. In my view, the briefer the pleasure the more heightened the thrill. There's nothing new in that. It's what men have been telling women for years.

2003

Cuppa Plenty

Most gardeners could not get through the day without the cup that cheers. Or preferably the mug. Or several mugs. Gardeners and tea go together like wheelbarrows and manure, or spades and wellies.

Of course, there are those who prefer a cup of coffee, but the die-hards, the traditionalists, the real men of the soil, know that *Thea sinensis* rather than *Coffea Arabica* was put on earth so that Adam the gardener and Eve the plantswoman could have an excuse to lean on their hoes from time to time and contemplate the fruits of their labours – forbidden or otherwise.

I came to realise that a mug of tea was the dynamo of the potting shed forty-odd years ago when I started my apprenticeship on the council Parks Department nursery. At home, tea was something dispensed from Mum's classy, contemporary, stainless-steel teapot into her pale green 'Beryl' china cups. The sort that the WI uses down the village hall. Mum did not realise this was the case, having always spurned the WI because she thought all they did was "argue over the teapot". The 'Beryl' was packed off to a church jumble sale as soon as she realised it was a bit common, and replaced with something by Denby.

But on the nursery there were no such niceties. The tea was made in a brown enamel teapot and brewed and brewed and brewed until it could melt the bowl off the spoon that stirred it. Dick Hudson, the tractor driver, would then decant it into his pint pot, lace it with Carnation evaporated milk, stir in four spoonfuls of sugar and down it between chesty coughs and deep draws on his Capstan Full Strength. He'd then lope down the yard on his bandy legs and climb into his tractor cab, fortified for a day's mowing in the riverside gardens. Well half a day really. He seldom left the nursery before 10 o'clock, having clocked in at eight, and would return at three to hose down his gang mowers and settle into the brown and battered uncut-moquette armchair in the smoke-filled mess room for yet another restorative brew and half a dozen fags. His rattling cough could send pigeons flapping for cover.

Not that he had gone without his brew in the interim. The Thermos flask in the metal box at the side of his tractor would keep him going during the rest of the day, but you could tell that its contents were a poor substitute for the steaming white porcelain pint pot, which, when emptied of its contents, would remain the same colour as the tea that once filled it.

He tried to clean it one afternoon. With Vim. He failed. Even the nation's number-one cleaner could not remove the ingrained tannin from Dick's pint pot. The rest of us gave it a wide berth, fearful of the germs it might contain, though, truth to tell, the strength of the brew probably gave it germicidal qualities.

The rest of us tried to set an example, by having slightly less sugar and washing our more modestly sized mugs thoroughly after use. We would use the same Brooke Bond or Typhoo, but our tea never came out the same colour as Dick's. Maybe he was more generous with the bags.

Tea still plays an important part in my day, though Dick would have a few words to say about my namby-pamby preferences nowadays. The wife is woken up with a cup of Earl Grey; I'm happy with a blackberry fruit tea in the morning, but really could not do without a Lapsang (no milk and on the weak side please) in the afternoon. Oh, and I like it in a china cup.

Yes, I know. Call myself a gardener? It should be Tetley full-strength if I want any kind of street cred. And where is the evaporated milk? Or, even better still, the condensed milk. That was Dick's greatest treat. It was thick and white, with the consistency of impact adhesive. I tried it myself once (from my own mug, not Dick's) and nearly threw up.

But each to his own. I know that come the witching hour – be it 11 in the morning or three in the afternoon – nothing else will do. No amount of freshly ground coffee or diet cola or bottled water that has spent 2,000 years travelling through solid rock and which must be drunk before September 2007 will ever usurp tea in my affections.

The ritual boiling of the kettle, the warming of the pot, the spooning in of the tea, the filtering through a strainer and waiting for just the right moment to decant my perfectly brewed cup all add to the anticipation of a moment or two's pleasure while I survey the assiduously weeded and deadheaded border.

Ah yes! Perfection. And then it is over and I can go back to work.

If they ever ban the drinking of tea in public places, there will be a riot. But it looks unlikely. Mind you, I don't suppose it will be long before someone tells me my Lapsang is bad for me. I tried to find it when I went to China a few years ago. I thought I'd bring back a packet of the real thing. They'd never heard of it in Shanghai, even though I asked for it in my best Chinese accent. Instead, the shelves were full of Lipton's. Funny that.

2007

SEPTEMBER

The Great Survivors

There will be one newspaper headline that you will never see. It runs something on the lines of "Wildflowers doing well; no cause for alarm." I suppose it wouldn't be classed as anything worth telling people about. No shock horror there. Shame really. After all, we have plenty of the "Plants in danger of extinction" stuff to make folk aware of the need to conserve, so wouldn't it be nice to hear things like: "Cowslip thriving, naturalists delighted"?

Well, I am here to try and redress the balance. My findings, you will understand, are not based on any scientific evidence, and not one survey has been undertaken to back up my views. All my opinions are based on personal observations and not one committee has been consulted. So you'll understand that my results must be reliable.

I'll begin with the cowslips. I've never seen as many as were decorating fields and roadside verges this year in my own part of Hampshire and on a run down to the West Country in early June. The fields were so thick with them that I thought they were buttercups.

Now, there is no doubt that this is due to the fact that farmers are much more chary about spraying their fields than they were in the bad old days of Rachel Carson's doom-laden book, *Silent Spring*. Thank goodness that early warning system was sounded but, perhaps now, 30 years on, we could allow ourselves just a little celebration.

The hedgerows in Cornwall should be a part of it. This summer, they were just like herbaceous borders. If you've never seen a Devon bank or a Cornish hedgerow, you don't know what you're missing. They are quite high mounds of earth that are backed by drystone walls and the cliff face of soil is simply plastered with wildflowers. These range from red campion and buttercups to meadow cranesbill, bladder campion and foxglove, with blue and yellow vetches tossed in to add to the wonderful spectacle. Just drive down a West Country lane in early summer and you'll feel as though you are passing between twin herbaceous borders, but when do you ever read about their beauty? Have you ever seen May blossom as prolific as it was this year? The hawthorns in my neck of the woods were absolutely dripping with foaming cream flowers, and the blackthorn that preceded the May was wreathed in white like a spring bride.

There will be those who tell you that this foretells a hard winter to come. Rubbish; it reflects a good summer just gone, when all the wood was beautifully ripened and more flower than usual was produced as a consequence. And there you are again. We had plenty of headlines about the late spring and not one about the subsequent spectacular eruption of blossom.

Enough of the moans. It's just that I thought someone should sing the praises of our wildflowers, especially now children are taught that they are not to be picked but to be conserved. The trouble with this is that conservation seems to be practised from a distance and this means that children, although trained to respect those inhabitants of hedgerow and field, and mountain and moor, will never really get close enough to know them.

I recently unearthed a pressed flower collection that I'd made at school when I was eight years old. An old scrapbook revealed page after page of crisp little sprigs with names like green alkanet and fox-and-cubs, hedge woundwort and black medick, all held in place with stamp hinges and identified in spidery script, courtesy of my first ink pen. There were 96 of them, which means that when I was eight, I knew almost a hundred wildflowers.

Maybe that contributed to my passion for gardening. What I can't believe is that it contributed to the depletion of our wildflower population. Nothing was picked if it was the only flower of its kind in view, and there were no roots attached to any of the crisp remains. What this pilfering did produce were children who knew their basic wildflowers as well as children today know the cast list of *Heartbreak High*.

What we need is a resurrection of the pressed flower collection. Children, and grown-ups come to that, need to start picking bluebells and foxgloves and looking into their drooping bells and spotted throats. Yes, leave the rare orchids well alone, but enjoy the commoners.

Plants, after all, are great survivors. If the motorways fell into disuse tomorrow, in 100 years' time, they would be impassable, thanks to a jungle of wildflowers, shrubs and trees that had sunk their roots into the seemingly impenetrable surface. Wildflowers are tougher than you think and they'll be here long after we are gone. I reckon it's time we got to know them a bit better.

1996

A Walk on the Wild Side

As you get older, do your tastes become simpler? What's brought about this philosophical turn of mind? My wildflower meadow, that's what.

Two years ago, we were lucky enough to acquire a couple of acres of farmland backing onto our garden, with the specific aim of encouraging butterflies and bees. The problem with farmland is that it's rich in nutrients, having been sprinkled with fertiliser annually for centuries. Well, one century, anyway. Before that it would have been muck. But, either way, it's not the impoverished earth in which one is always advised to grow wildflowers – the danger inherent in rich soil is that the grass grows too vigorously and flowers are forced out.

We did at least start with bare soil, the farmer having obligingly ploughed and harrowed the ground, but it's surprising how undulating the surface still was – like the Yorkshire Dales in miniature. Anyway, we have a ride-on mower and a miniature chain harrow. It didn't completely even out the surface, but gave it the contours of Suffolk rather than Yorkshire.

I wanted to sow the wildflower seed in late summer so that through the winter it would be vernalised – frozen then thawed to trigger growth – which is necessary for certain seeds. And the mixture? We're on chalky soil, so I plumped for a suitable meadow mix from Emorsgate for chalk downland. A few days later, several large sacks arrived and it was time to get down to the pleasurable, if antiquated, task of sowing.

You may remember that a few years ago on *Gardeners' World* I sowed a small patch of wildflower meadow in a field above Barleywood. I used an old seed fiddle I'd picked up at a farm sale. Since then, it's been hanging in the shed, so I took it down, filled it up, and fiddled. And after five minutes it broke. Now the pleasure in using a seed fiddle lies in its simplicity and the smoothness with which it does its job. You pull and push the bow, just as you would with a violin. A leather thong spins the plate which distributes the seeds as they fall from the sack, which is tucked under your arm rather like a set of bagpipes. But when the thong jams in the pulley, it doesn't spin. It simply irritates you.

I tried to repair it and managed another minute before it jammed again. In the end I gave it up as a bad job and resorted to a plastic bucket and my hand, humming *We plough the fields and scatter* under my breath as I strode about.

I very quickly discovered that if you scatter seeds with your jeans tucked into your wellies, your boots end up full of seeds. So I smartly pulled my jeans over the tops of my wellies. Neat, eh? Except if you scatter seeds with your wellies tucked under your jeans, you get blisters on the sides of your calves and, two years on, I still bear the scars.

But the seeds did germinate, and last year I had a patchy greensward of wildflower plants and grasses. I knew from Barleywood that wildflower meadows come into their own in the second year, and so it has proved.

This spring and summer, up came crested dog's tail and cocksfoot, sterile brome and other grasses of whose identity I'm not certain, followed by salad burnet, marguerites and vetches, clover, wild mignonette, and then knapweed and scabious – an ever-changing tapestry of delicate native flowers. A sprinkling of yellow rattle applied last autumn has reduced the vigour of the grasses by parasitising their roots and weakening them.

And the butterflies and bees? Well, the bees have turned up in generous numbers – honeybees and buff-tailed bumblebees plus some with Dennis-the-Menace markings. My identification skills are improving. Butterflies have appeared, too. Not in clouds, but in sufficient numbers to make the whole exercise worthwhile. And I'm hopeful that the planting of native hedges on which they can lay their eggs will boost their numbers yet further in years to come.

So far, we have seen meadow browns and gatekeepers, ringlets and speckled woods, painted ladies and commas, large and small whites and the occasional blue. Peacocks, small tortoiseshells and red admirals still seem to prefer the buddleia in the garden but maybe they've not yet been round the back of the house.

I took my Keble Martin out with me last week and counted 75 different species of wildflower in my meadow – the ones that I spotted and could name – which leads me to believe that there will be the best part of a hundred different species all told. Walking among them is a rich and rewarding experience, and a reminder that we neglect our native flora at our peril.

2009

On Public Display

Phew! We finally did it. The garden was flung open the day before yesterday and I'm still reeling. You may recall that earlier in the year I burdened you with my worries. Well, after much deliberation and a family pow-wow or two we decided we'd give it a go one Sunday afternoon, between the hours of 2 and 6pm.

We decided not to do teas, you may remember. Then one lady wrote and said that the ladies of the local church should do it for us. If they refused we were to let her know and she'd write to the bishop. Thankfully, it didn't get that far. One of our neighbours rang to say she'd booked the village hall and she and her ladies would be doing scones and tea. The proceeds would be in aid of the same charity as our garden opening.

Then the local Lions rang up. Where were the cars going to park? In the village hall car park, was the answer. The Lions would provide us with signs and men to act as car park attendants.

Slight unease on my part. This thing was growing. Was the garden up to it? For two days beforehand, my lady-who-does-in-the-garden and myself worked flat out. Weeding, edging, mowing, prinking, pruning; we did the lot. Piles of stones were moved by hands blistered by besoms. Shrub roses were trussed to let people pass; signs erected to divert visitors from the non-scenic compost heap.

The night before, the man from the Lions rang. He hadn't seen any posters in the village. Would people know about the opening? I worried all night, lest the listing in the local paper and in the Order of St John county handbook had not been enough. I'd refrained from advertising any more for fear that we would be overwhelmed. Had I actually erred on the discreet side?

The day came. I woke to the sound of torrential rain. Eventually it stopped. At about 1.40pm cars started to appear and people were seen walking up the road. The garden became like an ants' nest as snaking rows of people clambered up our hillside. At 2.45 the car park started overflowing into neighbours' drives. Have you ever seen your garden absolutely full of bodies? It's quite a sight.

By 5.45pm it was all over. We'd been visited by 700 people. Nothing was pinched, nothing was moved. I have not found one cigarette end or one piece of waste paper. People left smiling and as I passed one lady on her way down the hill she grinned at me and said "Perfick!"

We are shattered and so is the garden. But after slaving over something for ten years, it is rather nice to show it off a bit. Would we do it again? You bet.

1991

Refining My Taste

Garden ornaments, I am of the opinion, say more about you than plants ever can. You see, you can put down the appearance of a spike of gladioli, a couple of French marigolds or a red cactus dahlia to a simple mistake, but when it comes to a plastic heron or a painted gnome, then the die is cast. You show exactly what kind of gardener you really are.

Now please, for heaven's sake, don't assume that I'm being at all judgemental. If your particular penchant is for painted pixies, then you jolly well stick to it, but don't be surprised if you look through the complete works of Russell Page, Sir Roy Strong and Sir Geoffrey Jellicoe and find them signally lacking in such embellishments. It seems that the grander gardeners don't rate these little folk. They would sooner see a Portland stone sundial or a sandstone obelisk.

Mind you, I do know that in Sir Roy Strong's garden there are several putti (not to be confused with putty which prevents the glass in your windows from falling out). I should point out that putti are cherubs. In terms of mythology in the garden, it seems that putti are acceptable but pixies are not.

Bizarre isn't it? I suppose I may as well come clean and admit that I, too, have a pair of putti (not to be confused with a pair of puttees which soldiers during World War I would wrap around their calves to protect them from the mud in the trenches).

Mine decorate the entrance to my rose garden (small but heavily perfumed). They recline in rather a *louche* manner and one of them protects its private parts with a bunch of concrete grapes. The other appears to have been given a length of concrete muslin to drape over a pair of thighs that would make Rosemary Conley wince.

Now you never encounter this kind of coyness in a gnome (not to be confused with a gnomon which is the pointer on a Portland stone sundial). Gnomes push wheelbarrows, fish, and stand with their hands on their hips wearing expressions of abandon, unlike my putti which at best look rather sickly, and at worst positively inane.

From this you can deduce that the gardener with gnomes (not to be confused with gonads, which have quite a different purpose altogether) cares little for the pretentious scorn of those who appear over the fence and poke fun at his brightly painted garden ornaments.

I remember watching a television programme once that showed all manner of very eccentric front gardens filled with modal villages, representations of the entire British fleet, a replica of the Crown Jewels and a complete bathroom suite where nasturtiums trailed down the front of the bidet (not to be confused with something you wash your feet in).

I have a sneaking regard for those gardeners who fill their plots with sea shells or box bushes that have been clipped into the shape of steam trains, battleships and elephants, even though one of them came a cropper a few months ago when he was accused of sculpting something rude from a yew.

Apparently, he explained to the magistrate at the hearing that although it offended his neighbour at the time, it would be a thing of beauty and a joy for ever once it was finished.

It seemed that in its early stages of development the piece of topiary work resembled something not altogether savoury, bearing in mind the exclusivity of the area in which it was being created.

You can bet your bottom dollar that the complainant was definitely a putti man and not a gnome man. I'm only relieved that my topiary (not to be confused with a toupee which is false and hairy) was created round the back of my house, well away from public view. The prospect of having to display my taste at the front of the house for all to see is too risky by half.

I'd rather keep folk guessing as to my taste until I know them well enough to invite them round the back. By then I don't care if they are into cherubs, cheeky chapppies, stuffed storks, plastic trellis or solitary topiary (not to be confused with sola topi which stops the sun going to your head).

Better by far to have no ornaments whatsoever, then you cannot be confused with anything.

1994

Pondlife

We've got a pond. Well, we've got two ponds actually. One is small and round with a cherub fountain in the middle (don't make that face – it's not nearly so naff as it sounds) and the other is bigger, more natural looking and is meant to be a wild-life pond. It's about 25 metres by 15 and I am tempted to call it a lake. Well, to be honest, I do call it the lake, if only to differentiate it from the round job with the cherub holding the dolphin spouting water (no, it is not naff).

But there are problems with a wildlife pond. (I'll go back to calling it a pond now in case you think I have ideas above my station and that the pleasant chap who used to present *Gardeners' World* now clearly has an estate the size of Rutland. I don't. It's only a couple of acres.)

The problem with a wildlife pond is that wildlife uses it. Yes, I know this should not come as a surprise when it was clearly the sole intention, but the wildlife starts using it before you are ready.

We excavated the hole in the autumn. We built banks, lined the pool and covered the whole thing with soil before adding the water. We let it settle for a few weeks and then we added some plants. Not huge ones. This is a large area of water and so I bought lots of small plug plants thinking, in my ignorance, that it would be cheaper in the long run.

It was not. A pair of mallards, with an extra male in tow, discovered the water quickly. It is, after all, only the other side of the lane from the village pond where two geese, one swan, several coots and a dozen mallards regularly disport themselves.

They glided in and examined the rather smaller version of their primary residence and did a recce of the likely food prospects. The tiny plug plants were uprooted with little ceremony in the birds' search for food among the succulent compost that surrounded the roots.

I spent the rest of the winter, and much of spring, rescuing small plants of yellow flag iris that were floating out across the pond, their roots having been dislodged from the soil in which they were lovingly bedded. Some have grown away well, but the unfortunate ones are still struggling.

But at least the tadpoles have done well from the frogspawn donated by neighbours. Huge they are. They line up in the shallows, their broad snouts (do tadpoles have snouts?) pointing at the bank, and then dive for cover in great shoals as I walk around the pond.

We introduced newts, too. Well, efts to be precise. Lovely word, eft. Very handy for crossword compilers. They'll be big newts by the summer if the heron doesn't hook them out.

I haven't seen him yet, but I've seen his footprints in the shallows. Massive they are, but then I suppose they have to be. If you're going to spend a lot of time standing on one leg it stands to reason that the foot has to be pretty big, or you'd fall over.

You very quickly learn, when you have a wildlife pond, that you cannot be selective about the wildlife that uses it, you have to take the good with the bad. Not that I'm being judgemental. I've always thought the heron to be a remarkable bird, except when it takes my golden orfe. Still, there are no golden orfe in this pond.

But to sit on a bench and watch a newly created sheet of water turn into a living, breathing community is a pleasure like no other.

Pond skaters arrived within days. Water boatmen followed. We now have diving beetles. Dragonflies have been prospecting for egg-laying sites, and I still get a thrill from watching grey wagtails dabbling in the shallows, blackbirds splashing as they bathe, and swallows skimming the water for insects or for a drink.

I always feel a great wave of satisfaction when a robin perches in a tree I have just planted. The feeling of vindication that comes as a result of making a wildlife pond is a hundred times greater.

But there are limits. Two Canada geese turned up last week. We watched them for half an hour. I mused on the likely future of my plants. We walked round the pond and they flew off. I'm not sorry. Oh, they can come back, and cover the grassy banks with poo, but not until my plants are a little more established. I've got some bigger ones now. Bigger than can be lifted by your average duck. But Canada geese are burly brutes and I wouldn't put heaving a one-litre rootball past their gardening capabilities.

Now if the swan came over the lane from the village pond that would be a different thing. I think I would sacrifice my pondside plants for the sight of a swan gliding over the water.

It reminds me of the conversation I once overheard at the RHS Chelsea Flower Show. Two aristocratic ladies were walking down Main Avenue. "Do you have swans on your lake?" asked the one. "On the large lake, yes," replied the other. Now there's something to aspire to. As yet I do not have a swan on my large lake. But I do have a dolphin in my small pond. And it is very tasteful.

2005

Texted to My Limits

Birthday presents are not what they used to be. Time was when you could look forward with reasonable certainty to a monogrammed hanky or possibly even a pair of long grey socks. You knew where you were then: bored but with a clean nose and warm feet. Children, in those days, might just remember what brand of aftershave their father used, usually Old Spice, but that was as far as their imaginations carried them.

But this year my youngest daughter clearly decided that smellies and socks would betray lack of imagination on her part. She set out instead to improve her father's vocabulary. Not the vocabulary used in everyday conversation, as she often complains that my daily patois is, if anything, too rich in the rhetorical department. It was in another area of communication that she decided I was wanting.

The text messages sent by me to her mobile phone were, she thought, at best staid and at worst downright dreary. In order to remedy the situation she bought me a little red book, which is a dictionary of text messages offering me a chance to make my communiqués shorter but brighter and give me a chunk of street cred at the same time.

I have it in front of me now. The one message with which I have greatest sympathy is TIADD2M, which means This Is All Double Dutch To Me. Mind you, these nifty little abbreviations do make texting a darned sight quicker than when you are trying to spell out every last syllable. It's far quicker to say TGr8C than Take Great Care, or WerRU? instead of Where Are You? Fathers do, on occasion, need to ascertain the whereabouts of even their grown-up offspring.

There are, to be perfectly honest, loads of textual abbreviations that I can never see myself having cause to use and which my daughter would find baffling if I did. I'm quite sure that she is as clueless as I am when it comes to deciphering ISMAP, the Integrated System for the Management of Agricultural Production (EU), or FEEA, the Foreign Exchange Equalisation Account. But I think I must also take care to avoid using the more colourful little phrases that might imply a familiarity unbecoming in a father-daughter relationship, such as IS★★WenUXMe, which means I See Stars When You Kiss Me. Mind you, I'm more worried by the fact that she might be using that one to communicate with someone else.

But with the odd agricultural acronym thrown in, I did wonder if gardeners could not develop their own texting shorthand. It would be fun to be reminded to W8NTLORTM2PLNT. Wait Until Autumn to Plant, or CTLWN2CEAWK, Cut Lawn Twice A Week. Imagine the delight of a neighbour who is looking after your garden while you're on holiday. You could text daily with those little reminders that will prevent disasters befalling your precious plants. WHaBOAD, Water Hanging Baskets Once A Day, or PFF, Please Feed Fish, could help to cement that neighbourly bond in your absence.

But it's here that my little dictionary could pose problems, for I might not agree with its translation. While to me PANDORA means Please Allow No Dogs On Rose Arbour, anyone with my little red book will assume I'm talking about Prototyping A

Navigation Database Or Road Network Attributes. The local Labradors will be clueless.

Similarly, an innocent remark to a helpful neighbour could easily be misconstrued and might lead to serious complications. Take SINBAD, which I would use when offering watering instructions for my ferns, meaning Stand in Bath All Day. What happens when my unattached neighbour translates this as Single Income No Boyfriend Absolutely Desperate? Or the equally innocent LMIOTS, meaning Lawn Mower Is Outside The Shed, which could be translated as Let Me In On The Secret. It could lead to a KOTL, Kiss On The Lips, or a GYHOMA, Get Your Hands Off My Assets.

Clearly this new system of communication is something best left to those of junior years. I'd rather stick to the fountain pen and the Basildon Bond and leave my daughters to the pleasures of texting. You see, I've just looked up CRAFT in the little dictionary. Apparently it stands for Cooperative Research Action For Technology, but alas at my time of life it means something completely different. It's an acronym associated with those things known as senior moments. It stands for Can't Remember A Flipping Thing, which is how I'll be with the text messages should I forget to carry my little red book.

2001

Old Friends

Chatting with Roy Lancaster recently, we both became dewy eyed over childhood memories that were triggered by particular plants. Roy recalled an elderly lady berating him when he was young for referring to a snowdrop variety as Sam Arnott. "Did you know the gentleman?" she asked. "No," replied Roy. "Then how dare you address him so familiarly? He is S Arnott to you, or Mr Arnott." Picture one young plantsman put firmly in his place.

Happily, most plant memories are less likely to give rise to a cold sweat. My first ones are triggered by Beatrix Potter's *The Tale of Peter Rabbit*. Not just the blackberries, lettuces and cabbages, though these are vivid enough. No, I love the sight of a white-edged pelargonium (is it 'Frank Headley' or 'Flower of Spring'?) falling victim to Mr McGregor's boot.

Then, in *The Tale of Jemima Puddleduck*, there are the foxgloves in the woodland glade where the foxy-whiskered gentleman lures Jemima with a promise of somewhere safe to lay her eggs. It is for this reason that foxgloves always make me shudder a little, but in a fond and pleasurable sort of way.

With their glistening, succulent seedlings of microscopic proportions, mesembryanthemums remind me of the day I first sowed them as a ten-year-old. My dad, unaware of the location of my seedbed, trod in the centre of it, and my young plants germinated with a clear footprint in the centre of the clump.

Then there were plants to be afraid of. The cuckoo pints or lords and ladies growing in the wood was one. Its location was a bit of a give-away. It always skulked in the bottom of a tangled hedgerow as though trying not to be seen. Its flower looked sinister, with that black finger sticking up in the centre, as if beckoning any unfortunate child who had not heard that it was deadly poisonous. If you dared to cut open the flower, as I finally did at the age of eight or nine, you would find a collection of little flies trapped in the chamber at the bottom. Oh yes, clearly this was a wicked plant.

Bramley apple trees have happier associations. They remind me of Mr and Mrs Cawood at the bottom of our street. They had a monster Bramley in their garden. Nothing else grew in this narrow strip of ground, just long grass and buttercups and a few clumps of nettles.

The Cawoods hardly ventured down there except once each autumn, when Mrs Cawood would hold the stepladder and Mr Cawood, never sure on his pins, would totter to the top. He would then shake the laden boughs with the crook of his walking stick, sending the weighty apples thumping into the grass, and occasionally giving Mrs Cawood a bruising. For the rest of the week the tang of stewed apples would drift through their open back door, and we knew that the harvest was being preserved for the winter.

Old Mr Wright at the bottom of the street wanted no such work. It was he who saw the sign on my gate saying "Mint 1d a bunch." He enquired of my mother while I was at school to ask whether he could have some.

My mother agreed, however she declined his penny, feeling that a commercial instinct was unhealthy in a boy of nine. She failed to spot the fork that Mr Wright held behind his back.

He dug up the entire clump and disappeared. I saw neither my mint, nor his penny, ever again. I still treasure those early days of buying plants. My first bedding was bought in wooden trays from the local nursery, and the trays returned after planting out the contents. My first roses came from Woolworths, the coppery-salmon 'Helen Traubel' and the rich red 'Ena Harkness' with her weak neck. 'Sterling Silver' was a real let down, a dingy lilac, but I did like the multicoloured 'Masquerade'.

If travel broadens the mind, then so do plants, for at the mention of a name they can take you back to your first encounter. In the same way that I can close my eyes and walk around St Mark's Square in Venice, so too can I enter the greenhouse at the Parks Department nursery and smell those chrysanths. I can also sense the earthy humidity of the fernery, as steam belched from the iron heating pipes that had just been drenched with water from a hose.

I remember buying apple trees and a weeping willow from a nursery that's now a development of town houses. I don't think such dreaming is a sign of maturity. It's an awakening of earlier pleasures. A plant with whom you've had a relationship for a number of years is an old friend and when you plant it, years later, it's as welcome a pleasure as having a drink with a mate.

2003

OCTOBER

Home Is Where the Heart Is

I'm not especially happy about being away. Not for long at any rate. It has taken me ages to work out why, and I suppose the answer was staring me in the face. It's because deep in my innermost self, like it or not, I'm a gardener. And yet my anxiety is not based on the fact that my garden will go to rack and ruin. I know that the plants will carry on without me because I have a bit of help – Sue has been with me for around 20 years now. She knows how I garden almost better than I do, so it's not as if I can blame my unease on the lack of watering and weeding.

And yet there is always this deep-seated feeling that I might miss something. Perhaps it's as simple as that. Gardeners are tenders and carers. We function at close quarters with our charges – reading their moods and catering for their every whim. And so when we are distanced from them, there is a feeling of apprehension that, on our return, even if all is well, we'll not be quite as on top of things as we were when we left – that our relationship with our plants will have suffered.

This insecurity is not imagined. Whenever I am away for a few days, I prowl around the garden on my return seeing what has come out and what has gone over, making a mental note to snip this back or stake that – things that would have been attended to without a second thought had I been in residence but which, because of my absence, seem to assume a false importance.

Maybe I'm just too much of a control freak. Even Vita Sackville-West, the chatelaine of Sissinghurst, said that by August her garden had blown itself and she was happy to go away to some other exotic location while it dried up in the summer sun. I wish I could be so *laissez faire*. My garden ain't a patch on Sissers, but I can't bring myself to turn my back on it at any time of year.

Occasionally I'm offered a television series that would involve being away for a couple of months, filming in exotic locations. Much as the offers are tempting, there is simply no way that I can come to terms with such a prolonged absence. It's not that I don't trust those that I leave behind to keep the plates spinning on top of the sticks. It's not that Mrs T would be unhappy (though I like to think she might miss me more than a little), it is quite simply that, as someone rooted in the earth, I find the very thought of that kind of absence inconceivable.

Ah well, there goes my chance of being the next Attenborough. Intellectual capabilities aside, I fall at the first fence in terms of availability and, as Woody Allen famously said: "Ninety per cent of success is turning up."

Perhaps my anticipated anxiety is a direct counterpoint to being here in my garden on those perfect days: the first warm summer mornings when I can take my bowl of porridge to the seat overlooking the wildlife pool, and wake up as I watch the dragonflies flitting over the glassy surface. Or in the early evening, flopping down with a glass of wine on the same seat, I can marvel at the swallows gliding in to slake their thirst on the wing – scooping up half a thimbleful of water without crashing into the plants at the waterside.

In March I can watch hares boxing on the barley field at the back of the house while I wheel rose prunings to the compost heap for shredding. On summer evenings I can sit in the swing seat, dozing with the cat and breathing in the scent of lavender. In autumn there is that nostril-biting, bittersweet aroma of fading foliage and crushed chrysanthemum leaves, and my neighbour's bonfire smoke that I admit I love to hate.

Winter brings the moaning of the cattle on the farm next door, brought in for the miserable months. At harvest time it is the drone of the combine, followed by the whirring of the grain drier in the silos. There is the roar of the mower, the snip of the shears, the scent of crushed foliage and fresh compost, of roses and pinks, of narcissi and lilies, and the lemon-mousse aroma of *Magnolia grandiflora* on the side of the house. Each of these occurrences may take only a moment in the gardening, and farming, year but if I missed any of them, I would feel deprived.

AE Housman remarked in *A Shropshire Lad* that, "Now of my threescore years and ten, twenty will not come again". Alas, 50-odd of mine will not come again, which leaves me "little room" to look on "things in bloom". I'm not being morose, you understand. Just practical.

The recollection of these simple, often fleeting pleasures reassures me that I'm happiest at home, on my own patch, with my own piece of earth. I shan't give up the shorter trips. I don't want to become xenophobic. And yet I don't really understand those people who travel "to find themselves". Me? I was here all along.

2007

Thinking Big

There's nothing like a bit of garden visiting to sharpen your appetite. We went to stay with friends in Dorset last week-end. He's a garden designer, so you can imagine how I felt as we departed Hampshire and drove west. There was, within me, that eagerness and curiosity to see what he had created, mixed with the merest hint of unease. It was a certainty that within half an hour of our arrival I'd be depressed at the high standard of his creation compared with mine.

Now I don't want to sound discontent. I'm very happy with the plot *chez Titchmarsh*, and with my own modest efforts when it comes to landscape architecture, but I do occasionally turn the colour of grass when I see a garden that I really covet, and owned by that rarity – a garden designer who is also a plantsman.

This turned out to be one such. It was made on many levels that rose up on slopes stretching away from the house, and it had all those things that design-conscious gardeners dream of – pleached allées and formal rose gardens, a long canal stuffed with water lilies, clipped evergreen oak standards, obelisks of yew and box and a wonderful butterfly meadow a-flutter with common blues and silver-washed fritillaries.

The beauty of this garden, apart from its breathtaking design, was its variety. There was an overriding formality – a definite shape to the areas, courtesy of stone and gravel, but also a freshness to the planting.

The main formal area outside the back door was composed of two rectangular gravel gardens where, among a few strategically placed shrubs and the hard lines of stone paths, the likes of aquilegias, verbenas and bupleurum were allowed to seed themselves. The hardness of the lines was softened by the looseness of the planting.

Pots were strategically placed – but not always in the obvious positions. This gave the garden an unexpected "kick" – a bit of edge. It set us talking – the garden owner and me – about the successful elements of design in a garden and it struck me more forcibly than ever before that it is almost impossible to over-structure a garden.

It could simply be my own taste of course (I've always been a bit of a control freak when it comes to line and form, and the axis of paths and vistas is usually my prime concern), but this garden epitomised all I love about gardens. It also spurred me to be bolder.

For a start, I love clipped box and yew, but I know now, from what I saw last weekend, that I could afford to use larger plants. My own box lollipops are perhaps a foot and a half in diameter. My box balls are the same dimension. I know that in time they will grow, but I could easily plant standards now, like holly and *Ilex crenata* and even the evergreen oak, much larger than that – say four feet or even six feet across.

"Hang on a minute," I hear you say. "What about the budget?" Of course, there is the element of cost to consider here, but one can always buy smaller plants and let them grow if resources are restricted. It was not my budget that had kept me thinking small where my topiary is concerned. It was, if I'm honest, my mind. Perhaps I was afraid of "going large". Not any more. So I have come home armed with ideas that I can use to change my garden this autumn and give it a bit more drama. I have plants in pots on my terrace but the pots are about 18in across. I am about to order some that are three feet in diameter and stuff them with hostas and agapanthus.

It's all to do with scale, you see. On a small back doorstep there would be no room for such hefty containers. But on a terrace or a patio almost anyone could fit a 3ft pot planted with one of these two summer beauties. And the impact they create is far and away greater than containers just half that size.

I have an idea to improve a long, 4ft-wide border that runs in front of the terrace. I want to position some of these large pots at 8ft intervals along it and plant in them either olive trees (I've had three of them outdoors there for five years now and they've not turned a hair) or an evergreen, such as the aforementioned ilex.

With a row of these large pots and their statuesque inmates as the prime feature, I could plant lower-growing perennials around them and give the border much more drama. It will cost a few bob, but the plants and the containers will last for years.

What is so heartening about visiting good gardens like the one in Dorset is that they can sharpen your appetite and give you renewed inspiration for your own plot. How I would love a canal or a rill. Can I fit it in? Where would it go best? Well, we can all dream, but if my visit makes even a part of that dream reality, then my garden will be better as a result.

I do love gardening. I love the fact that every so often I feel like a kid again when it comes to freshness and enthusiasm. I'd never get the same sort of thrill out of golf.

2006

Grumpy Old Gardeners

Gardeners are such happy people, they never complain, do they, said a lady of my acquaintance. I don't know where she's been all her life, but that is certainly a myth.

I always used to think that gardeners were the optimists and farmers were the pessimists. Ask a farmer about the weather, or his crops, and he'd say that things would only get worse. Ask a gardener, and they'd tell you next year everything would be much better. Nowadays, I'm not so sure.

I was taken around a friend's garden recently, and while I was marvelling at the flowers on this and the blossom on that, she kept up a commentary about the state of the slug damage, the effect of the birds, the drought, the running to seed of her onions and the damping off of her courgettes. I came away feeling really quite depressed.

So whatever happened to those gardeners who were so cheery? The fact is that they've probably never existed. Look at the likes of McAllister, head gardener to Lord Emsworth in PG Wodehouse's Blandings Castle novels. Now Lord Emsworth is my hero, a man who wants nothing more out of life than to lean over the door of his pigsty and scratch the back of his prize sow, The Empress of Blandings, with a stick. His gardener, on the other hand, is a man with flame-coloured whiskers and a temperament to match. The garden belongs to him, not to

Lord Emsworth, and flowers must not be picked or bedding schemes changed. So where is the sunny temperament in that?

He is probably of the same clay as Beatrix Potter's Mr McGregor. If ever a young child were keen on gardening, one brief browse through *The Tale of Peter Rabbit* would certainly put him off for life. Here is a man who hates rabbits, birds, and probably his employers and the rest of humanity into the bargain. Sunny of temperament? Humbug.

You can watch keen gardeners gradually decline, you know. They start off light-headed and jolly, discovering the simple pleasures of sowing seeds in finely raked earth, and rooting a first cutting. Then, as their enthusiasm grows, they take the weight of the horticultural world on their shoulders and suddenly it all becomes a deeply earnest chore, with twenty rows of potatoes to harvest in July.

And then look what happens if you try to employ a gardener. He'll have back trouble and be unable to do heavy work. He'll start late and finish early. He won't let you into his greenhouse until he's gone home for the day. His tea breaks will be longer than his working hours. He'll want a rise every couple of months. You'll return home from work and not even be able to see what he's been doing.

But, just a minute. What am I doing? Grumbling, that's what. There you are, you see: it just goes to prove my theory. Gardeners are a miserable bunch.

1993

Losing the Label

How we love labels. We like to label people; he's the strong, silent type; she's the blonde air-head, and if we're gardeners we like to label plants. Now I try very hard not to attach labels to people, knowing how I hate them attached to myself, but when it comes to plants I'm in something of a quandary. If I don't label my plants then how can I remember what they are? I can call most of them to mind, but there are always the odd few that elude me. New plants always take a while to get to know really well, so I do still need a gentle reminder.

I know well that there are gardeners out there who are hugely organised, to the extent that they have a map of their garden with all the plants plotted in. All they have to do when a friend enquires as to the identity of a specimen, is look up in their diagrammatic ledger the precise location of the plant and regale them with its full moniker. There are even people who use their computers to perform this service. Well, I am not of their number.

"But just a minute," I hear you cry. "What's wrong with labelling your plants?" Well I do; but I don't label them quite as obviously as some gardeners do. I have never found labels to be intrinsically attractive things. Oh, I know there are people who have bright white tags sticking up behind every last seedling in their garden, but I have always considered this sort of arrangement to be highly dispiriting. Walking into a well-labelled garden can create the feeling that I am in a cemetery and every headstone is in place, even before the plant has actually died.

At a place like Kew Gardens I can understand it: we go there precisely for the reason of learning about plants and identifying them with ease. The labels at Kew are black with white writing and offer all sorts of intriguing facts as well as the plant's name. They will tell you the family the plant belongs to, and its country of origin. They may tell you who collected it and when, and they will even bear an accession number which allows botanists to look it up in their own ledger, which is now, no doubt, on a floppy disk, and fill in its background.

I worked at Kew once. There were two students there who were mad on rhododendrons. They could refer to particular plants by their accession number alone. Conversations were run on the lines of "Have you seen that *R. sinogrande* at the foot of the dell?"

"You mean 8573-stroke-49-stroke-KW-stroke-19?"

"Yes."

"They're going to move it so that it's nearer 8756-stroke-44-stroke-EW-stroke-5."

I have to admit they both had anoraks with fake fur on the hoods. It turned me off labels for life, but not rhododendrons.

In domestic gardens these black-and-white engraved sandwich labels, as they are called, would be prohibitively expensive, so some other means must be found that couples efficiency with subtlety. The plant must always be the first thing you see and not the label.

I loved those old Victorian lead labels that were engraved by using a special machine that would stamp its letters deep into them. They were often used in alpine houses and were a dull silver-grey that could be easily read; making them practical, but not obtrusive. Alas, they are no longer manufactured.

For trees I do have an aluminium die-stamping set which, when I have some spare time on long winter nights, I do occasionally get round to using, but the operation is tedious as it takes one clout of the hammer on the die-stamp for each letter. When you find yourself having to engrave a label for *Clematis viticella* 'Purpurea Plena Elegans' you really do feel like throwing in the towel as it can take almost an entire episode of *Inspector Morse*.

What I tend to do now is write on a small, anodised aluminium label in soft pencil and push this down into the soil behind each plant, when I find a suitable site for it in the garden. I try to leave about a quarter of an inch of it protruding so that it can be pulled out in any moments of lapsing memory. But such labels always seem to get hopelessly lost. Either the plant grows over them, or I have mice that are collecting them. For whatever reason they are quite often impossible to locate.

Maybe I will simply have to adopt the technique of an old gardener I used to work with. If ever he was asked to identify a plant whose name had temporarily slipped from his memory he would cough a little to give himself time, and then, when his memory was clearly going to let him down, he would say, "Ah, that's *Avantaclewia*. Yes. *Avantaclewia damdifino*. Tricky blighter."

1996

Looking for Dove

Unless they are in a pie, I have never been partial to pigeons. Don't ask me why, but peristeronic pleasures have always eluded me, apart from the pleasure of using the word peristeronic. Peristeronic is to pigeons what bovine is to cows. Not a lot of people know that; even fewer care.

But there are those for whom a garden would not be a garden without the clatter of pigeon wings, or the cooing of doves. I am not of their number. I have only to look at a pigeon to be reminded of the mess it leaves behind. Trafalgar Square is, for me, an orgy of ordure.

I lived in a bedsit when I was a student, and the landlady seemed very sniffy about my tank of goldfish. It wasn't a large tank, and it only contained three fish, Clapham, Tutin and Warburg, named after the authors of a British flora book. But she wasn't that attached to them. Not that I had much time to be attached to them either; they died within a month and then went on to supply nutrition to a rose at the bottom of my landlady's garden.

But, strange as it seems, she was quite keen for me to get a couple of doves. "I wouldn't mind them cooing on the window-sill," she said. All I could think of was the mess. Her plan came to nothing.

Why doves? I guess she fondly imagined that they'd strut about on her guttering, taking off with a round of applause to circle in the blue sky above, before returning to decorate the sill, in more ways than one.

But there are moments when I take stock of the situation and ask myself if I really wouldn't like to have a few fantails for my garden. After all, they do look rather sweet when they puff out their chests and display their tail feathers like a hand of cards, cooing their liquid notes to female doves, who sit on the shelf looking gormless.

But what nearly persuades me once or twice a year is the display of dovecotes at Chelsea and Hampton Court Palace Flower Shows. These elegant, white-painted homes on poles, equipped with more doors than Buckingham Palace, do look handsome. You can almost see one of them in your own garden with the doves coming and going, if not with olive branches in their beaks, then at least with a song in their heart.

It was at one such moment of weakness that I found myself gazing upwards toward the dovecotes at Hampton Court, the vision of white feathers and blue sky swimming in my mind's eye. And then the conversation taking place between the salesman and a potential customer insinuated its way into my daydream.

"How do I clean out the droppings?" was the question. "Oh, you just have to put your hand through the openings and rake them out," came the reply. No, thank you.

But I do still like the look of a dovecote. After all, these peristeronic palaces do grace the gardens of some of our finest stately homes; there's a wonderful granite-built one at Crathes Castle, near Banchory in Scotland.

Grandly designed farmyard barns have dovecotes, too, frequently with row upon row of entrances and exits finely crafted in complex brickwork. You can see them in the gable ends of elegant 17th and 18th century houses. The crinolined ladies must also have been pigeon fanciers, unless those portals were there simply to allow access for the bearers of love letters: all part of the peristeronic postal system. But then, how did they get up there to relieve those little pink legs of their little purple passages? Perhaps they climbed ladders in their stockings.

The other day I saw a white-painted dovecote in a garden in Sussex. I thought how nice this particular pavilion on a pole looked, and that perhaps I should invest in one after all. But what was it about this dovecote that I found so attractive? The penny dropped. It had no doves in it. I looked more closely. The reason was simple, its holes were not holes at all but painted on with black lacquer.

I think I have just sold myself a dovecote. All the pleasure of a fine garden ornament with none of the by-product. All I need now is a blue sky. I'll forgo the clapping wings.

1995

Plants I Have Loathed

There are those who assume that because one is a gardener, one loves plants. It's not an unreasonable assumption, but then it's akin to suggesting that all musicians love music. Neither statement is true. In the same way that musicians appreciate some kinds of music but not others, gardeners have a passion for certain plants and a loathing of other kinds.

Now the thing about this hatred for certain members of the plant kingdom is that it's always irrational and usually based on nothing more than blind prejudice. Me? I have a problem with pampas grass. Don't ask me why; it must have something to do with the fact that I got fed up with seeing it billowing from a small lawn in front of a house near the nursery where I worked. It just sat there, and every autumn it squirted up its silvery plumes like an umbrella stand full of feather dusters. The house was probably occupied by a fanatically house-proud woman who liked even her garden to be spotlessly clean.

I know it looks spectacular, but what does it really do except sit there and squirt?

Perhaps this is the key to my plant hates: I have a problem with anything that looks unyielding and immobile. Cacti might come from the baking desert, but they leave me cold. Gladioli might be majestic and sword-like, but I will happily cut them dead.

Now this is completely unreasonable. Cacti, for instance, were some of the first plants I grew from the school bring-and-buy sale when I was a nipper. They sat on the window-sill of the upstairs loo for years. Doing nothing. There was one cigar-shaped job that put on an inch or two of growth every year, but that inch or two got thinner and thinner so the plant began to look like an emaciated sausage.

I suppose the lavatory window-sill is not the most appropriate place for a plant with this sort of habit, especially if one is having problems in the regularity department. I forget what happened to it in the end. It probably gathered so much dust that it expired due to an inability to photosynthesise.

It's appalling really. Call yourself a gardener and then allow plants to die through lack of interest? Definitely. I'd do the same today with that grisly little waterside plant *Houttuynia cordata* 'Chameleon'. Have you seen it? Its leaves are a mixture of red, yellow, cream, green, brown and goodness knows what else. The plant clearly can't make up its mind what colour it is and so has decided to be all things to all men. Well not this man; you can keep it.

I feel the same about a lot of purple-leafed plants. Now some, like *Cotinus* 'Royal Purple' which I have underplanted with grey-leafed lamb's ears alongside my garden shed, looks stunning. But then the hybridists started thinking that there should be more purple-leafed plants and they came up with *Physocarpus* 'Diablo'. Aptly named, I reckon. It's diabolical. And it's not purple at all, just a mucky brown; if I want to look at that colour I can go and stare at my compost heap.

Then you have diascias. These are lovely little things when there were about half a dozen of them, but have you seen how many varieties we have now? About 16,000 at the last count, and every darned one of them the same shade of pink. I like diascias, but not that much.

Of course, what one must account for is changing emotions. There are plants that one falls out with, having been partial to them in the first place. This is often due to them getting bigger than their boots. A plant that develops a rampant habit and which is determined to take over more of the garden than you are prepared to let it have, soon becomes an arch enemy. Mind-your-own-business is one such plant. So is that chocolate-spotted hieracium that now erupts from every damn crevice on my terrace, along with the wand-like linaria with purple spires of flowers that can find purchase in the smallest pocket of soil. 'Pink Chiffon' opium poppies are going the same way, as is the red orach. Like borage, you only need to sow it once and it will be with you forever more.

But then I have a sneaking admiration for these survivors: they might be rampant, but they lack the smugness of the plants that I really hate. And that's it, that's what I really loathe in plants: self-satisfaction. I want them to look as though they actually care about where I put them and where I plant them, and to appreciate my care and attention.

Nothing is guaranteed to make you love a plant more than a tricky patch when it looks as though it's going to die and then recovers. Such a state of affairs shows that a plant has gratitude. I like that. I'll continue growing a plant that doffs its cap, gives me a wink and thanks me for growing it. And what thanks do you get from a cactus? Just a nasty little prick in the finger.

1997

Greenfingered, But Not Greenfaced

Garden envy ... does it really exist? I was contacted by a national newspaper a few weeks ago and asked for my opinion. I expressed the view that in general, while gardeners would sigh over gardens they considered worthy of high praise, their feelings seldom ran to out-and-out jealousy. I mean, we're far too gentle a breed, aren't we? Surely we would never covet our neighbour's plot, even though we might be just a teeny-weeny bit envious, on occasion, of a well-tended lawn, a well-grown row of onions or – as happened to me this year – a massive Chinese dogwood in full flower at the side of the road. It was not that I wanted to uproot it and cart it away, but it did send me off in search of a suitable specimen to plant at home.

I suppose that was the nearest I've come to envy – if you don't include Stourhead, Studley Royal, Chatsworth and Helmingham Hall. But, you see, here we are talking about things that are way behind my reach. I am unlikely ever to own a 'Capability' Brown landscape or a stately home, so envy would be quite pointless. And yet, when I gaze on a beautiful landscape – almost always involving trees, grass, water and a classical building – there is, inside me, a deep-rooted ache. A kind of longing I suppose. It's not, I would maintain, a longing to own such a landscape – it's more of a longing to be in its presence, which some would argue amounts to the same thing. And yet, I've never really thought of it as envy.

Envy is what you feel when you are entering the local village show and your neighbour's parsnips are longer and better grown than your own, even though you share the same soil. Ah! So it does exist among gardeners then? Well, in extreme cases, yes. We've all heard stories of sabotage: of prize pumpkins and marrows being slashed with knives or smashed with a hammer. But I would like to think that none of my readers is of this vindictive persuasion. True gardeners would be spurred on to do better by such eventualities – and to do their best to coax out of the champion grower, his or her recipe for success. (That's not envy, that's pragmatism.)

But we all strive for perfection to some degree, whether it be a hole-free hosta, a blight-free potato or a weed-free lawn. The joy though, is in the creation of such perfection, rather than the simple acquisition of it. Mind you, if I were offered a

'Capability' Brown landscape tomorrow, I would jump at the chance to keep it looking wonderful. Which leads me on to taste. You see, not everyone rates 'Capability' Brown. There are those who think he was a vandal; a one-trick pony who desecrated the British landscape and swept away many fine formal gardens in his quest for Arcadia. There are also those who envy his landscapes not one bit and who would happily replace them with herbaceous borders, parterres and topiary. (Mind you, they'd need quite a lot of the stuff to cover the ground that Mr Brown covered.)

On a smaller scale one might admire a bedding scheme or a bed of dahlias but, generally speaking, such feelings would simply spur one into doing better on one's own side of the fence, not because of envy but because of inspiration. The Chelsea Flower Show has a similar effect. I know that many folk leave the banks of the Thames in May feeling that their plot will never measure up, but they are also fired with enthusiasm to have a go at something new. You could never call it envy.

I tried my best to give the lady from the newspaper the copy she wanted, but I could tell, by the end of our conversation, that I was signally failing to satisfy her journalistic appetite. Nothing short of bloodthirsty avarice would have placated her. Rather than tales of pure revenge and retribution, of slavering covetousness, all I could do, feeble gardener that I am, was to say that if one of my neighbours has some superb plants in his garden, I am happy to lean over the fence, congratulate him and ask for the name of his liquid feed.

I never did see what she wrote and I doubt very much that I was a part of it. She no doubt settled instead for a litigious dispute over a leylandii hedge which had led to blows with at least one party being sent to prison. I explained that if Leyland cypress is properly clipped once or twice a year, it's no problem at all and makes a very good boundary. But her attention had wandered now. She might even have dozed off. A gentle murmur was all she could manage.

In the interests of being interesting, I think I need to go on a self-assertiveness course. If it succeeds, you'll read about it in a newspaper . . .

2009

NOVEMBER

A Garden Is for Living

Some interviewers ask the most impertinent questions. "Have you ever made love in your garden?" enquired *The Observer* recently. Don't get excited. You're not going to get an answer. Well, not a proper one. I'll tell you the same as I told them: "Not in this garden. I've only just moved."

It's funny, though, the implication that making love out in the garden is daring. I suppose it is if you live on an open-plan housing estate. You'd have to choose your moment very carefully: half-past three in the morning would be my suggestion. The dirty stop-outs should have rolled home by then and the early risers will still be a-bed.

Better, though, to find a dense shrubbery. Or perhaps a narrow grassy path between towering flower borders where the perfume of lilies or mock orange hang heavily in the air. No! You see, it's so easy to get drawn in.

And yet, the less risqué tactile possibilities of a garden are relatively unexplored. It is the simplest of all pleasures to walk across a finely mown lawn in bare feet, but gardeners tend to traverse their grass in stout footwear, wellies or walking boots. This is no way to enjoy the sensation of early morning dew as it washes the digits of your pedal extremities. June might be better than November, but hey, give it a go. It is wonderfully liberating.

So is cleaning out a pond. Now I do find this a bit of a chore if I have to do it in bare feet, but some folk positively relish the feeling of mud squeezing up between their toes. I prefer a pair of chest-high waders, through which I can enjoy the pressure of the water without getting wet. Working between flowering water lilies that are within sniffing distance is a rare treat.

At this moment you could be starting to worry about my predilection for the unusual sensation in gardening. Not to mention the proximity of rubber. But what are you, a boring stick-in-the-mud or a daring sensation seeker?

Well, settle for something between the two and climb a tree. Yes, I know, the last time you climbed a tree you were in single figures, but have another try. The views of your garden even ten feet up are almost as thrilling as those to be had from riding in a hot-air balloon. You don't like heights? Rig up a harness and a rope, then you can enjoy the sensation without risking life and limb. Better still, risk life and limb!

"Irresponsible," you cry. "Yes, thank God," say I. We live in an age where the Princess of Wales Fountain manages to stay open for less than three weeks before it is closed because somebody slipped and bumped themselves. I mean, what are we coming to? I gather conkers have now been banned in schools.

Can we bring an element of common sense to bear please? Can we just say to folk that if they fall over and hurt themselves in a public park that has been reasonably maintained it is their own fault for being clumsy and not looking where they are going? Hard-hearted? Not a bit of it. It is the only way we will get life to return to normal.

The paddling pool on the Yorkshire moors where I grew up is now empty of water. In my day it was surrounded by mums and dads with children sailing boats and pond yachts, with little girls paddling, skirts tucked into their knickers. Now it is deserted, probably on account of health and safety. The trouble is, health and safety never took account of spiritual enrichment. You can be as healthy and safe in body as you like, but if your mind is stultified what is the point?

At least in your own garden you can have a water feature to splash in and a tree to climb. Yes, of course you must be careful where children are concerned. Small children can drown in very little water, but they can also experience untold joys there, and do things that they will look upon with affectionate reminiscence when they are older.

Oh, listen to me going on. Well, I feel pretty passionate about it, that's all. If we lose our ability to enjoy excitement and physical sensation, then we lose the ability to live life to the full.

In our gardens we should be able to do more than simply a little light weeding, or sitting in a chair looking at it. We should paddle in water, walk around with bare feet, climb trees and, well, your private life is your own, but if you want to do what the man from *The Observer* was going on about, do it quietly, round the back of the buddleia.

Life is for the living, pools are for the paddling, and trees are for the climbing. When we forget that, we'll be a sad lot, and the only people not complaining will be the lawyers.

2004

As One Gate Closes . . .

Moving house. Two words that can conjure up fear and dread in the hardest of hearts. Moving garden. Even worse. If you're a gardener that is. Well, here we are after 20 years, the missus, the kids and me, uprooting ourselves from Barleywood and moving to pastures new. "Why? What's wrong with that lovely garden that's taken you years to make?" people ask. "Absolutely nothing," I am forced to reply. So why am I going? Because it's time. It may seem like a lame reply, but I know what I mean. Maybe you do, too.

It won't be easy, saying goodbye to a garden that I've made from scratch. People ask if I am digging up lots of plants to take with me, and look at me as though I am barking mad when I say that I am not. But then, you see, I made a garden at Barleywood, and I want to leave a garden behind, not a patch of earth full of holes. Hopefully the people who take it on will appreciate it for what it is and go on to put their own stamp on it. The last thing I want to do is to rebuild the same garden around a different house. What would be the point of moving?

So why are we really going? Well, I wanted to make one more garden, preferably around a period house. We've found a Georgian farmhouse just three miles from where we live, so our social life need not change. It's not a grand dwelling with porticoes and pillars, just a handsome, mellow-brick affair that needs a bit of re-pointing and re-roofing, with a front that looks as though it should be hinged like a dolls' house. And the garden is surrounded by a brick and flint wall. A walled garden! Well, you can see why I'm excited.

So what sort of garden will I be making? Well, one that suits the house. Pyramids of clipped yew, long flower borders, that sort of thing, but I don't want to overdo the box hedging.

It will be interesting to see if I can give a Georgian garden a bit of a modern twist without it looking out of place. I don't want the garden to appear closed in and over fussy, but I will still want to grow masses of plants. And I do like making stripes on a lawn. Perhaps, at last, I'll have a cylinder mower rather than a rotary. Simple pleasures, eh?

Of course most people, on moving, would make sure they had better soil than they were leaving behind. I'd like to tell you that I am most people. Alas, I am not. It's the same sort of stuff, chalky and flinty. But I'm taking my manure heap with me and I know fertility is not too far away. There's no great slope at the new place, so that will make cultivation a tad easier as I get closer to my dotage, but there is no greenhouse either, so until I get one I'll have to make do with hardy forms of propagation. And yes, I have been madly rooting cuttings through the summer.

This is beginning to sound like one of those Christmas round robins that offer unwanted information on families that you have hardly seen for years but as you've been coming into my back garden for the best part of 20 years, first with *Breakfast Time* and latterly with *Gardeners' World*, it seems right that you should know.

We'll be keeping the woodland above the old garden so that we can watch the trees grow and see the bluebells every spring, but my biggest worry is the cats, Spud and Hector. They'll still have plenty of room to wander, as the two acres at the new place are surrounded by farmland, but will buttering their paws really stop them from trying to cross town and make their way back to the garden that has been their home for four years? We'll see. And I shall worry until they settle.

I shall never forget it. The seaside garden and the Far Pavilion, the safe haven of the potting shed, the tranquillity of the lily pool and the warmth of the Mediterranean garden. And my greenhouse. Oh yes, I shall certainly miss my greenhouse. But this is no time for melancholy. It is a time to look forward and to remember pleasantly. Must go. Pots to pack, cats to find, new beds to dig. Heigh-ho.

2002

Trowels and Tribulations

Life is just a bowl of cherries, says the song, and who am I to argue? The trouble is that if you're a gardener some of your cherries always get pinched by the blackbirds. Irritating isn't it?

To be fair, most of the time I find gardening a rewarding sort of business, but every now and again a fly lands in the ointment of my horticultural life and drives me right up the garden wall. The all-time least favourite of the things that are sent to try me is the kinking hosepipe. It does not matter that the manufacturer promises me it is nylon reinforced and guaranteed to be easy to use. Oh no. Just when I've got to the far end of the greenhouse, furthest away from the tap, or when I've pulled the hose around a corner in the garden, it kinks and reduces the flow by three-quarters, accompanying the abatement in supply with a loud hiss at the tap end. This indicates that, due to the increased pressure in the hose, water is now escaping through the tap connector.

Now my hosepipe may be unpredictable in its kinking but in one aspect it is unfailingly reliable: the moment I reach the kink, which will be a couple of feet away from the tap, it will blast off the hosepipe and soak me with water. It never fails. I have had more wet legs than a fisherman.

And that's another thing. Wellies. Wonderful things. I'd never be cast away on my desert island without them. Until they leak. And when do you discover that they leak? Just when you decide to clean out the garden pond. Don't bother to bale it out with a bucket, just keep wading out of it and emptying your leaky welly. And another thing: it is always the right foot, never the left.

When you've refilled the pond you will, like as not, discover that it, too, now has a leak, and if you thought that finding the hole in a punctured bicycle inner tube was difficult, you've clearly never tried to find the hole in a pool liner. It equates, in the fascination stakes, with watching paint dry. And so to drier irritations, like deadheading. As a pastime I quite enjoy it, until I come upon that one crisp and faded flower head which I cannot reach, way at the very top of the stem of a rambling rose, just outside the bathroom window. I know; I'll leg it up the stairs, open the window and snip it off from there. You've guessed. It is just out of reach. Only an acrobat from the Moscow State Circus could remove it with his Felco's, and that's only if he could rig up his own trapeze from the window-frame. I do not number such a performer among my close acquaintances. The result is that the crisp and faded flowerhead remains in place, with its finger to its nose, until the gales of autumn finally bash it into submission.

All these problems and I haven't yet got on to pests and diseases. They all irritate the pants off me, but there is one pest that bugs me more than any other, and that is the fast-moving slug. Yes; I know that slugs are not renowned for their speed. We are not talking about the Ferrari of the mollusc world when we mention the slug, but just watch him go if you plant out a tender morsel one evening and forget to take anti-slug precautions.

By the following morning that plantation of tobacco plants will be as perforated as a teabag or as filigree as a pair of net curtains. His little legs may not move fast but he has a pair of gnashers that would not disgrace a piranha. And don't let them tell you that slugs don't have teeth but a rasp-like tongue called a radula. Utter rubbish. They have dentures that make Sir Les Patterson look like a toothless old crone. They must have, how else would they wreak the damage that they do? As if the animal world could not provide enough problems for the gardener, we have to invent machinery which can beat nature into a cocked hat. There is the lawnmower that refuses to cut the sticky-up-bit of ryegrass right in the centre of the lawn. There is the lawnmower that refuses to cut evenly, one side of the blade is somehow higher than the other. And there is the lawnmower that refuses to start at all.

We have the pair of secateurs that have been cunningly designed to cut almost-but-not-quite through the stem so that the portion of growth you are removing manages to tear away some of the parent stem, and the Dutch hoe which has been systematically programmed to seek out the soft and tender shoot of a lily or other emerging choice plant among the weeds with all the efficiency of a heat-detecting ground-to-air missile.

With all these little vicissitudes of life to cope with, it's a wonder we don't throw in the trowel. And if mine bends once more when it hits a stone, that's exactly what I shall do. With great force.

1997

Don't Ask Me!

I think that as far as the national press is concerned, I must be a bit of a disappointment. You see, they ring me up from time to time for a comment about the current state of the weather – a cold winter, a late spring or a scorching summer – expecting, or rather hoping, that I will confirm their suspicions that we are on the road to ruin and that our gardens will never be the same again. During this last hot summer these phone calls came particularly thick and fast.

Now let's be perfectly honest. It's very flattering to be consulted for one's opinion on almost anything – the implication being that the combination of advanced years and careful reasoning have imbued one with a kind of rationality that is rare in those with less experience.

And yet I cannot help but feel, in moments like these, that I am found wanting. I'm at the stage of discovering that the older I get, the less sure and certain I become about almost everything – not least the value of my opinions. It is a sad state of affairs, an affliction I suppose. But in spite of the fact that folk of apparently greater intellect than I are prepared to make unequivocal pronouncements about everything, from global warming to the emission of greenhouse gases, I find myself unable to line up with them. It's not that I disagree with what they're saying, or that I am cavalier about our treatment of the planet. Quite the reverse. The stewardship of our natural resources and the countryside are, to me, the two greatest priorities in life. But if experience has taught me anything it is that nothing is certain.

No two summers are ever alike, and while the general trend over the last few years may have been for less rain and higher temperatures, that doesn't necessarily mean that over the next few years the trend will be the same.

In the Middle Ages, the weather was so mild vineyards were planted as far north as Yorkshire, yet in the 17th century the River Thames froze to such an extent that 'frost fairs' were held on the ice. The weather patterns over our island have always been fluid. The real news would be if they did not change.

It's a known fact that the earth wobbles on its axis and that in doing so, it wobbles away from the sun and then closer to it. This would account for the contrast between medieval vineyards and the frost fairs.

I don't doubt that the industrialisation of our planet has a bearing on our climate, and we must do everything in our power to keep such effects to a minimum. But to say how much we ourselves are affecting global warming can only be educated guesswork, and I've never been good at guessing.

There is no shortage of people who are prepared to tell you exactly what will happen if we continue the way we are now, and those who are given the most column inches are those who predict the worst-case scenario. After all, these pronouncements make better copy. They also imbue those who make them with the kind of gravitas that implies great learning. Pessimism has always been more highly rated than optimism – it smacks more of perceived reality. But it doesn't make it any more truthful.

This summer came a prediction from someone in authority that our lawns would soon be a thing of the past, that our weather would be too warm for grass as we know it and that we would have to seek an alternative. Our lawns would soon look like the fairways on Spanish golf courses with their thick tufted grasses, or we would have to change to clover. Why? Because this summer had been a bit dry during June and July in the south and south-east.

I was asked to comment. Was it true that soon we wouldn't be able to grow dahlias and delphiniums, that they'd be replaced by cosmos and hibiscus and that lawns would disappear?

I am a gardener in the south-east. In dry weather I do not cut my grass as short as in damp weather and as a result it stays greener. It did start to look a bit sad, but in the first shower or rain in August it instantly regained its usual lustre. I had a fine first crop of flowers from my delphiniums in spite of the fact they were not watered during the hot weather. I cut them to the ground after flowering and they gave me a second flush of bloom. My dahlias are sensational and, no, I didn't use a hose-pipe on them.

I visited Harrogate at the end of the summer where The Stray, a large acreage of greensward at the heart of the town, was as lush as can be. In the West Country, in the north of England and in Scotland they have no problems with water supplies or strawy grass. They must wonder what all the fuss is about.

So you'll forgive me if, when the next crisis occurs, you hear little from me on the likely effects. It won't be that I am disinterested, or that they forgot to consult me. It will most likely be because I came up with an answer that didn't make very good copy. And that answer was probably "I don't know." But at least I'm honest . . .

2006

No Place for Games

Sport and gardens do not go together. No, there is no persuading me. I've been around round objects long enough to know that unless they are called tomatoes or apples they do not belong in the garden. Families with small boys have my deepest sympathy, as the sight of that spherical object on an efficient trajectory to the greenhouse is much more than I could bear.

And yet I was a boy myself once. Back then we did not play football or cricket in the garden, we played it at the bottom of the street against the bus garage wall, stopping to allow the odd van or lorry to pass by. You could score 20 runs between cars in those days, nowadays you couldn't hear the scorer call your name above the din of juggernauts. Sad really.

Having two girls and no boys has made my sporting life a lot easier really. One of them was a swimmer in her earlier years, even got to Crystal Palace, but she never had the nerve to ask for a pool at home. Well, not seriously. We haven't really got the space, and anyway we have three ponds already. I offered on more than one occasion to let her do a couple of lengths in the large pond but she seemed unimpressed. Probably due to the duckweed. I can see her now, rising up out of the water in her rubber hat and goggles, coated in green like some monster from the deep. She doesn't swim as much now, so I'm glad I never invested in all that chlorine and turquoise paint.

The other daughter does play some basketball at school, but so far I have resisted the appearance of one of those white boards with a netted basket that are attached to house walls. Why is it that they only seem to fit in the most prominent of places, usually next to the satellite dish? I must sound like a miserable old dad. I'm not really. I'm just grateful that I haven't been asked to turn my garden into a sports complex.

Oh, there are some sports that lend themselves more than others to a garden setting, and we do dabble in croquet on the two sunny Sundays we seem to get each year. At other times, when I've cut the grass, I get out the hoops, the mallets and the balls and arrange them on the lawn as a sort of tasteful Edwardian sculpture. None of us knows how to play properly, even though everyone knows that it's a "cruel game" that's favoured by vicars with a sadistic streak.

I have toyed with a putting green. Nothing outrageous, just a finely mown sward and a red flag. But digging a hole in my lawn? Maybe not. Putters shouldn't do much harm, but my next-door neighbour who is a golfing fanatic might take an interest and he could be straight round with his Big Bertha and mashie niblick and before I knew where I was it would be divots a go-go and I would be regretting the fact that I'd ever heard of Tiger Woods.

A Frisbee, perhaps? No. It would surely decapitate the dahlias. How about kite flying? Nah. The string would only get tangled up in the oak trees. Archery looks quite pastoral, but you know as sure as eggs is eggs that someone who is not the best shot in the world is almost certainly going to impale one of my chickens before the day is out.

Some gardeners get around this problem by dividing their plot into sections. One for the kids and their ball games, and the other for adults and their more sedentary pleasures. But you know full well what will happen. They will have been playing for five minutes at the most before that ball comes spinning over the great divide and lands slap bang in the middle of your gin and tonic.

But things really become serious when the little Einsteins start experimenting with flight. They can send model planes buzzing around your ears, and they can even send up rockets to photograph the garden so that they can see you in the altogether on the sun lounger from a dizzy height. And then you have the problem of all that garbage in space. It's not high enough to go into orbit with all the stuff from the United States and Russia, so it comes down. And where does it land? Smack in the middle of your cold frame, that's where. So you see, it's just not on. The place for sporting activity is the local park, the leisure centre or the golf course, not the back garden. With the best will in the world I just cannot countenance the hitting or kicking or throwing of balls in the near vicinity of my plants or greenhouses.

But I smell trouble. My wife is a keen tennis player and the subject of having our own court has cropped up more than once in recent conversations. I think she's seeing how the land lies. Well I can tell her. It's a one-in-four slope, and that means lots of JCBs and earth moving. And you know that they won't keep to the farm track, they'll be over my lawn with their tyres before you can say love-all.

Nope. Monopoly. Now there's a nice and simple game, on a table on the patio. No problem.

2000

Defending My Shed

I'm an incensed man. I've just read a newspaper article telling me that sheds are the province of men intent on escaping from reality. Apparently the shed is a refuge for the exasperated male, full of useless junk and of little solace to anything except a mechanically-minded squirrel.

Fully determined to refute this infantile argument, I strode out to my shed, opened the door, ducked under the 'King's Cross' enamel railway sign, fell over a roll of wire netting and began to investigate.

Mine is a workshop replete with all those necessaries which a gardener must call upon: seven rubber and/or pruning voles, a pyramid heap of bamboo canes in assorted sizes, two large empty hanging baskets (didn't get round to planting them up this year) and five lawn mowers (only one working but the others will provide much needed spares). You see, some gardeners lack this foresight.

I will pass over the usual tools possessed by all men of the soil (the soil miller, the swoe and the beck) to remind you of the need for 18 roofing slates, 43 plastic sacks, two wicker baskets and 5½ dozen seed trays. What would I do in spring without them?

Where would I be without my coils of wire should something fall apart, or my dismantled fruit cage should I be visited with a plague of blackbirds?

The set of legs for a beehive and the two sides of a garden bench are merely waiting for their other halves to materialise.

Admittedly, the purple floral curtain lying in a corner is a bit of a puzzle, but the pink towel hanging behind the door next to the cowbell is vital when I spill petrol on my hands.

No gardener could manage without three containers full of nuts, bolts, screws and washers, or a length of kinked hose. One day it may have to be unkinked to replace the better stuff that's presently attached to the outside tap. But throw it out? Sheer folly.

I admit that I may be on more shaky ground with the empty milk crate (but it is handy for reaching the back shelf of the shed) and the drawer full of . . . well, I can't actually reach that, even standing on the milk crate.

Perhaps I will give way on the broken radio. New batteries and well-aimed swipes with the milk crate have so far failed to improve its reception. But even so it gets a better reception than the one I'd give to the author of the article. She was female, of course. And so is my garden helper. Bet she's responsible for that floral curtain in the corner.

1991

The Art of Mundanity

People ask me if my wife is a keen gardener. In reply, I smile sheepishly and admit that she is not, swiftly countering it with, "she enjoys looking at the garden and we discuss the creation of new features before I make them." To be honest, it's not something I have ever really felt strongly about. Having gardened, written about gardening or broadcast about gardening every day for the last 20 years, the last thing I want to do when I get home is talk about it all night.

I find myself wondering if Mr Smith is a keen cook. I can't imagine that he is. I mean, consider the prospect of sharing that conservatory with Delia and putting the whisk back in the wrong drawer. She might look calm as she folds in her egg whites on camera, but I bet there's a bit of seething temperament in there somewhere. Best that we don't know about it.

Not that so-called experts have a monopoly on lines of demarcation. I know that husbands and wives all over the country divide their gardens up into his and her territories, and woe betide one party if it steps over into the other half.

At BBC *Gardeners' World Live* in Birmingham and at other shows around the country, I'm frequently buttonholed by a wife and then apologetically shuffled up to by her husband. "She's the gardener, really," he confesses, "I'm only the boy." So, it seems that the distaff side of the family decides what will be planted and where, while the macho man mows the grass, clips the hedges and sweeps up the leaves.

Everywhere man is in chains and women wear the trousers. Not that men appear to grumble. Many seem happy with the lot of the serf when it comes to gardening. Well, I suppose that if you're a neurosurgeon or a teacher, you're grateful if somebody else makes the decisions for a change, leaving you with the undemanding tasks of cutting the grass and strimming the edges.

There are times when I am of their number. There's nothing I like better after a tough week of decision-making and rampant horticultural creativity than standing behind a lawnmower as it makes neat stripes up and down the green sward.

However, let not the female of the species persuade you that this is a job devoid of skill. Oh, no. Those lines have to be kept straight and it is no easy task. How is it done? In the same way as a farmer ploughs the land. It is something that comes with experience, as a farmhand discovered when he asked the farmer to reveal the secret. "Fix your eye on an object in the distance," the farmer instructed, "and keep looking at it while you plough. Then you'll get a straight line." The lad set to work and the farmer left, returning half an hour later to see how he had got on. The furrows were all over the place. There wasn't a straight one in sight. "What did you do?" asked the farmer. "I did as you said," replied the lad. "I kept my eye on an object in the distance." The farmer asked which object. "That cow," came the reply. You see, there's more skill needed in mundane tasks than you think. Brute force and ignorance are not enough. Even the most unskilled job involves its quota of aptitude and specialist knowledge. Take leaf sweeping. A simple task on the surface, but it requires knowledge of thermodynamics and hydrostatics.

Sweep the leaves in the wrong direction and what happens? They blow back at you, all over the garden. What began as a quick tidy-up could take hours. You must always sweep in the direction of the prevailing wind, using the force of the air to help you round up the foliage. Sweep towards a corner where the leaves are penned by fencing or hedging and the final gather, to use the terminology of BBC 2's former *One Man and His Dog*, will be completed successfully.

However, fail to account for local turbulence and your leaves will be scattered to the four corners of the garden. Rounding them up again will take more patience than is possessed by your average shepherd.

Then there's the sticky subject of moisture content. Try to sweep up the leaves when they are too wet and they cling to the path or lawn and refuse to be lifted. To enable a leaf to be removed from grass, tarmac, paving or even concrete, it needs minimum moisture content.

And there, gentlemen, you have it. The perfect excuse for not sweeping up those leaves at the first time of asking and one that, if given the detailed scientific explanation, your other half will be able to find no fault with.

Ah, yes. These jobs may appear to be unskilled to those with no scientific background, but we who are asked to undertake these seemingly mundane tasks know better. Growing plants? Pah, easy-peasy. If you want a real challenge, try mowing in a straight line.

1999

DECEMBER

Winter Tales

Winters have been funny things lately. Icicles have become an endangered species. I was talking to my 21-year-old daughter this morning about what winter means to her and she mentioned frost on leaves and wrapping up in warm clothes. She remembered a handful of snowmen from when she was little, but icicles? Not really. Snowdrifts? "Not in this country," she said.

It sets you thinking, doesn't it? It is not in my nature to be a doom and gloom merchant, shaking my head and muttering dire warnings about global warming. But I do think it's a shame that we don't have winters like we used to. I can say that, being a gardener. I'm allowed. I don't spend my winters standing on a station platform every morning because of the wrong kind of snow, or leaves on the line. Heaven knows what effect a real, proper winter would have on our transport system. We'd all have to work from home.

I can remember the winter of 1963 as though it were yesterday. I was still in Yorkshire then, aged 13. My home town of Ilkley nestles comfortably at the foot of the moors in Wharfedale, and kids from the outlying village of Langbar were not seen for several weeks. The snow was 12 feet deep in places. Sheep had to be dug out. Hay had to be airlifted to the fields.

How many children of today have listened to that echoing, deep hush the morning after snowfall, when cars and birds are silenced at a stroke? How many have seen trees stay white and snow-laden for weeks, rather than for a single morning? I'm not so much sad about it, as wistful. I loved those mornings, when you just knew it had snowed because of the reflected light that dazzled you from your bedroom window, even when the curtains were still closed.

As a gardener working at the local nursery, snow would be greeted with relief by gardeners who had had enough of winter digging of corporation flower-beds, and could look forward to a few days of desultory spade cleaning in an old, open-fronted shed heated by a brazier.

As an apprentice in the nursery, my workload changed little. The snow on the greenhouse roofs would soon melt, thanks to the warmth on the other side of the glass, and there were still plants to water, seeds to sow and pots to wash. Ah, that favourite of winter jobs. Scrubbing clay flowerpots in a tank of ice-cold, muddy water.

But for today's gardeners, snow is a worry. A heavy fall can damage evergreens, so we hurry out first thing in the morning to knock it from the boughs before it does any harm. Left until the thaw it can become so heavy that the wood snaps under its weight.

And yet the sight of snowdrops pushing up through snow is a real pleasure, even if it is rarely encountered. In a hard winter we are also comforted by the thought that the pests are having a tough time of it, and indeed, come the spring it does seem to delay their depredations.

Of course, they still have hard winters in Siberia and Finland and Norway and Sweden, and snow still falls on the ski slopes.

But I can't help thinking it's a bit of a shame that when you ask the youth of today what snow means to them they'll say Klosters or Gstadt rather than Kettlewell or Grimsby.

Snow has, you see, become a victim of fashion. Where once it fell everywhere in equal measure, it has now been hijacked by those resorts that have clearly found some means of wooing it in their direction. Snow has succumbed to commercialism. It is enticed by the prospect of people paying a fortune to glide over it on two strips of carbon fibre. Perhaps it also knows that in such a situation it will be appreciated rather than bemoaned. What other explanation can there be for its prolonged absence from the greater part of this country?

Of course, this winter could be an exception. But if we do get some decent snowfall, the kind that we remember having on a yearly basis when we were little, you can bet your bottom dollar that the papers will make a mountain out of a molehill. Global warming will have been forgotten, and the next ice age will be on its way. Before we know where we are, food will be in short supply and coal will be sold on the black market because central heating systems have frozen solid.

Call me a cynic if you like, but I'm laying in a decent supply of bed socks and nutty slack. You can't be too careful.

2001

The Great Escape

Just as a doctor or a policeman is never off duty, a gardener is never very far from the call of his watering can. Oh, it may well be December and the traditional season of peace, goodwill and putting your feet up by the cosy log fire, but the gardener's charges still make demands on his time. If he is within hailing distance of a leaf or a shoot your average gardener has feelings of responsibility which, from time to time, overwhelm him.

Now there are those gardeners who do not mind this state of affairs one jot. They are only too happy to be hostages to the hoe and slaves to the strimmer and, for most of the year, I am of their number. But there comes a time when I think that it is best for the plants and me to have a break from one another. Rather like the mother of a large family who loves her children to death, the odd few days without their company can do wonders to recharge her batteries and improve her relationship with them. It is for this reason that I really enjoy winter holidays.

At this time of year, with a breather from recording *Gardeners' World* and *Ground Force*, I occasionally allow myself the luxury of a winter holiday in the sun.

Not only are days off easier to grab when the garden slumbers, but the prospect of a bit of hot sunshine warming the back of my neck is irresistible.

Where to go? The Mediterranean is lovely but not much cop in terms of temperature at this time of year, so it is probably either the Canaries or the Caribbean. The Canary Islands have the advantage of being nearer to home, but the Caribbean wins hands down when it comes to tropical vegetation. Ah. Foiled. I'm trying to escape the garden and already the blessed flowers and plants are rearing their ugly, sorry pretty, heads.

Difficult isn't it? But I'll go along with it anyway. I have to confess that for me it is not simply the responsibilities of gardening that I wish to escape from, it is also other gardeners. There, I've said it. Now I don't want to be thought ungracious or ungrateful, but there are times when Oz Clarke and Jilly Goolden do not want to be asked which claret is the best value for money; there are brief moments when Delia Smith would rather not be asked about cranberries and limes, and there are, very occasionally, nano-seconds when I would really rather talk about anything other than gardening. Not very often, but occasionally. For this reason the Caribbean, being farther away from our shores, is more tempting than the more adjacent Canaries as it offers greater anonymity. I can definitely recommend Barbados with its wonderfully luxuriant Flower Forest and Andromeda Gardens, where exotic plants tumble down verdant hillsides to the ocean.

I'm trying desperately hard to think of white sand and blue sea and already images of flowers are seducing me, so perhaps I'll recommend to you Mauritius, which I visited last year, as being safer. There are fewer land-based gardens, but you can enjoy the underwater gardens among the coral reefs, best viewed from a glass-bottomed boat. The great thing is that there is no danger of you being asked to weed them.

We never think of the underwater world as being part of our province as gardeners. Yet when you've gazed through the glass at the bottom of the boat on an endless diversity of waving fronds which are strap-like and feathery, in shades of greeny brown and ruby red, you realise what an amazing world has been lurking out of your sight all these years. It is an escape from reality and a chance to disappear not only in the tropics, but also into your imagination.

There are moments though, even when I'm far away from it all, that the old face lets me down. I was deep underground in Barbados a few years ago, admiring the stalactites and stalagmites in a wonderful network of caves. There, clad in shorts, flowery Caribbean shirt and bright red hard hat with a paper napkin draped under it, as for all visitors in the name of hygiene, I was completely switched off and gawping upwards at the stalactites, when the man next to me whispered in my ear, "I bet you wish you were in your garden."

I smiled at him. He was wrong. I didn't. But I did wonder where I had to go to escape the pull of the soil. They say there are not many people in the Antarctic, but you can bet your bottom dollar that all the penguins watch *Ground Force*, and that at least half of them have a crush on Charlie Dimmock.

1998

All at Sea

On every gardening cruise there is a troupe of keen gardeners tucked away in luxury cabins, waiting for the moment to leap out and be amused as the ship sails to another port of call; and I am about to embark on just such a cruise.

It may seem like a doddle, this week of pleasure in warmer climes, where all a chap is expected to do is give a couple of lectures and answer gardening problems, but there is more to it than meets the eye.

It's not only during the question time sessions that you are expected to solve fellow passengers' problems. You'll be button-holed just as you are about to nod off, or just as that forkful of beef wellington is about to pop into your mouth. Perhaps the only place you can hope to get a break is in your cabin, but even there you are not immune to attack. My wife was amused on one trip when she noticed an envelope sliding under the cabin door. She opened it to find a note from a lady requesting an assignation with me to discuss . . . her rhododendrons.

And at each destination, as you disembark from the ship with keen gardeners in tow, you are open to another form of attack, known as the "what's this?" ploy.

I forget how many millions of plant species there are in the world, but I do know that you're expected to know each and every one of them as you journey round the botanical gardens of the world. It helps to have handy phrases such as "Ah, I'm not sure what they are calling this now, it's had so many name changes," or "it's an economic plant of indigenous origin, vital to the denizens of this island." At least this gives you a breathing space to search for the label.

Occasionally you'll hazard a guess and seconds later the wise guy of the cruise (there's always one) will unearth the label and say "that's not what it says here."

Then there's the weather. This is where agencies totally outside your control can ruin everything. After four days of solid rain on a trip to the Italian lakes, I was about to address the assembled party, when the tour operator met me outside the door, looking worried. "Make them laugh," he said, and left me to face the equivalent of a Monday night audience at the Glasgow Empire. They did laugh, eventually.

So you do your bit to enjoy the passengers' company and hope they enjoy yours. But every now and then you'll be reminded that you are there to work.

After battling against the elements on the Italian lakes tour, I staggered out of the airport with a suitcase full of damp summer clothes. As I left, a gentleman who'd been a part of the tour walked up to me.

How kind, I thought, he's coming to say goodbye. But no. He looked me squarely in the eye and said, "Huh; I don't know why you came along; proper waste of time," and bustled off. Which is why, occasionally, at the prospect of another gardeners' holiday, I break out in a cold sweat.

1993

Sharing the Garden

Two's company, three's a crowd they say, but in the garden there are those who think that two's a crowd. You see, gardening is such a personal thing that having two potterers tending the same border is akin to having two cooks in the kitchen. It's just that rather than fighting over the Aga, you'll fight over the agapanthus instead.

This fact was brought home to me recently by a couple who have his and hers parts of the garden. He's an ex-army man and his bedding plants, in primary colours of red, white and blue, are laid out with military precision, rather in the way that footmen at Buckingham Palace lay the table settings for a banquet. Everything is measured to the inch. She, on the other hand, is of the subtle school; tasteful combinations and pastel shades. The whole plot is a sort of Sandhurst meets Sackville-West and is not a happy union.

Talking of Vita Sackville-West, she and her husband Harold Nicolson were one couple who made a rare combination in the garden. He designed the layout of the garden at Sissinghurst and she masterminded the planting, allowing him to have the occasional look-in with things like the Lime Walk, or MLW as he used to call it: My Life's Work.

Other couples have a more uneasy relationship, like a household I know where the husband weeds a border, pulling out the offending aliens and leaving them on the lawn. His wife follows on, a couple of yards behind, putting back all the things he should not have pulled out.

Perhaps that's why, in many households, there are lines of demarcation when it comes to garden chores. More often than not, it is he who does the mowing, edging and hedge clipping, safe tasks as not much can go wrong there, and she who does the planting and the pretty things. Call me sexist if you like, but this is still the way that tasks are divided up in many gardens. It might not be politically correct but it works.

And yet, if you thought it was difficult gardening with your spouse, you should try employing a gardener or, worse still, taking on a garden that has resident staff. Oh it will all be very vague when you buy the property: "There's old Sam who comes in and does a bit for us; absolute treasure."

When you finally arrive you'll find that old Sam is Victor Meldrew incarnate; the original Mr Grumpy who regards anything outside the back door as his territory. You might have visions of billowing banks of old-fashioned shrub roses and violets, border pinks and lavender, but if he's grown scarlet geraniums, orange French marigolds, lobelia and alyssum for the last 20 years, there's not much point in expecting him to go pastel now. You've about as much chance of getting into his potting shed as you have of managing to get your saucepan onto top chef Marco Pierre White's hob. A snowball in hell's chance.

When the crunch finally comes and old Sam shuffles down the road grumbling with an armful of tools that will never grace your shed again, you will have to find a replacement. It is at this point that you are told that good gardeners are rarer than hen's teeth and that you'll be lucky to find anyone who knows the difference between a cauliflower and a cabbage rose at less than £20 an hour.

Don't you believe it; the gardener of your dreams is out there, it's just that you need some sort of dating agency to put you in touch. So many people get divorced from their gardeners nowadays that it is almost becoming the norm. One lady I know has had seven in as many years. She's known as Elizabeth Taylor at the local gardening club.

Far too many rose bushes, these days, come from a broken garden, but time can do wonders and if given the care and manure they deserve by their step-gardener they can recover and lead normal lives.

Should you try and patch things up when they just don't seem to be working out? For the sake of the plants, I think you should, but if it comes to a point where the dahlias are suffering because you argue in front of them all the time, then they are probably better off without you.

Divorcing your gardener can be a messy business, and you might be reluctant to give a reference that could woo another partner into thinking that they are the gardener of their dreams.

But it is only fair to remember that although you found them difficult to get on with, someone out there is simply made for them. When two gardeners of a like mind meet, they can make something that is bigger than both of them. The trouble is that you then need more staff, and the whole problem starts all over again.

God grant me a garden, but make it a small one.

1996

The State of the Gate

You can always tell when winter is approaching by glancing at the gardening diary columns in newspapers and magazines. The dead giveaway is when the writer, and I include myself here, starts to talk about applying coats of timber preservative to fences. Well, when you're on to that sort of subject there's clearly not much going on in the garden is there?

Oh, I know it's vital to make sure that the old interwoven doesn't crumble to dust, and that there is now a tremendous range of colours to choose from, but I still feel a sense of unease at recommending the operation. It may seem that I'm short of ideas of a more vibrant and horticultural nature.

And yet there is another consideration that I reckon is even more important than the state of your fences, and that's the state of your gate. The mood engendered by a gate can make or mar a garden.

Think about it. Consider the pleasure of a well-oiled well-balanced garden gate and then compare it with a tumble-down barrier held together by chicken wire and staples, with one broken hinge and two missing slats. You have to kick it to get it open, and then when you try to close it it traps your finger and gives you a blood blister the size of a small hen's egg. You're in a bad mood before you have taken two steps up the garden path.

A badly functioning garden gate is on a par with a fountain pen that will not allow its ink to flow smoothly, or a mobile phone that keeps losing its signal. Small irritations they may be, but they can make you more grumpy than you would believe.

Prosaic as it might seem, a garden gate is imbued with more than its fair share of romance. There are garden gates embedded deep in childhood memories: the intricate little wrought-iron one that Beatrix Potter's Jemima Puddleduck laid her eggs by; the white-painted picket one that Peter Rabbit squeezed under to get at Mr McGregor's lettuces, and the robust door-in-the-wall in Frances Hodgson Burnett's *The Secret Garden*.

Maybe you've always dreamed of a cottage garden with a white-painted picket fence and a gate to match, or a gateway adorned with an arch over which roses scramble. If that's the case, then perhaps it's time you made your dreams come true instead of risking a trip to casualty every time you battle through that broken-down wreck?

I speak with a degree of self-righteousness, having just fitted my garden with a wonderful wrought-iron gate. It gleams in lustrous black, it runs smoothly on its hinges, and it closes with a satisfying clunk. There is a danger that I may be certified, should anyone catch me standing by it at the moment. My face bears the beatific smile of Private Godfrey in *Dad's Army* as I repeatedly open and close it to enjoy the silken smoothness of its hinges and the satisfying sound of the catch. Go on, call me a simpleton, I don't care.

It operates so much better than the one at the other end of the garden, which has a temperamental catch that threatens to cut off my fingers every time I close it. There is one more gate in our garden. I found it a few weeks ago while I was weeding at the end of a wall where the nettles and brambles were waist high. It is a small gate, home made. The frame is of galvanised piping, which is not attractive in itself, but between this framework are horse's bits and stirrups, strange chunks of bridle and harness that have been welded on to make the inner part of the gate a little work of art.

It is rusty at the moment and in need of a bit of TLC. It will get it, not least because I bumped into a little old lady at the post office a few days ago. "Have you found your gate yet?" she asked. "The one with the stirrups?" I asked. "Yes. I helped make that when I was a little girl. I'm 92 now." I feel hugely proprietorial about my old garden gate and determined that the old lady's efforts should not go uncared for. The gate will come off its rusty hinges, be wire brushed and coated in gleaming paint and re-hung in the spot it has occupied for the better part of a century.

It may not have the romance of a Beatrix Potter creation, but for me it now has its own brand of special magic that is associated with our house. Somehow, I can't imagine feeling that depth of affection for a fence, whatever colour it is.

2003

A Chance to Unwind

There are moments in life when even the keenest gardener needs a little respite from affairs of the soil. Oh, it may occupy most of our waking hours, but every now and then, even the most dedicated son or daughter of the earth needs to rest and recuperate, to put aside worries about vine weevil and blossom-end rot and head off into the wide blue yonder.

I confess that I am never happier than when sitting on a bench admiring my own handiwork – the striped lawn, the billowing flowerbeds or the reflections on the surface of the pool. But then, like other gardeners, I know that such reverie will not last long.

It will be a minute, if I am lucky, before I spot the dandelion in the lawn, the twining stem of bindweed legging it up some tall perennial, or the blanket weed that's getting out of control. The result? I am up and out of the chair in search of the daisy grubber, the weeding fork or the wire-tooth rake with which to extricate the offending algae. Relaxation? Huh!

So it is just as well, if you are of the gardening persuasion, to have a hobby that takes you out of yourself from time to time. And one that takes you out of the garden, too. Especially in winter, when the seed catalogues have yielded up their excitement and there's nothing to do except wait.

Now if gardening is your only hobby you may well be harrumphing at the blasphemy implicit in this statement. Get another hobby? Well, I don't want you to see it as a replacement, rather as a counterpoint to all your graft in the garden. Something that will put it into perspective and allow you to return to the mower, the secateurs or the spade, refreshed and raring to go.

Me? I have a boat. Only a small one. It doesn't count as a luxury yacht. It's 7.5m long and pootles about the Solent with me behind the wheel. It's not a sailing yacht and as a result it attracts the scorn of those stick-and-rag men who have to wait for a breath of wind before they can make it from Lymington to Yarmouth. Unless, of course, they use the 'iron topsail' – sailor speak for an underpowered motor that can make two knots of speed against a five-knot tide coming in the opposite direction. You don't have to be a sailor to understand that this means you will go backwards.

No, with twin diesels beneath me, I have even more power than a ride-on mower and I can predict what time I'll reach my destination. That said, the last time I ventured out, the swell was rather larger than I'd anticipated and the boat and I came in for a bit of a hammering. There was seaweed on the roof by the time we reached the Beaulieu river.

But, you see, even then it was therapeutic and refreshing. I came back to my garden grateful to be on dry land and appreciative of the restorative properties of terra firma. They always say that the one infallible cure for sea sickness is to stand under an oak tree or, in my case, a chestnut.

Some gardeners dabble with vintage cars. Ah, now there's a dream. I look at the chrome on the 1929 4.5-litre Bentley Le Mans open tourer and wonder if I would ever cherish that as much as I do my Ransomes, Sims and Jefferies engine. (I lie – it's actually a Honda, but there is a musicality to Ransomes, Sims and Jefferies that the Japanese brand lacks.)

Come to think of it, music is a safer hobby. Especially if you combine it with gardening. If you play the flute or the violin, you can invite your musical friends round on a summer evening and play in the garden for their amusement. You love cooking? Great! You can cater for them, too.

But it's winter now and such alfresco reveries will have to wait. Better, perhaps, to make reading your hobby – it's cheap, it won't take up much space and you can do it on your own. John Le Carré is good, but avoid *The Constant Gardener*; it's not what you might expect. Steer clear, too, of *The Perfumed Garden*, which has little information on the cultivation of roses.

You'll be far better off tackling Ian Rankin or PD James. After a murder or two, you'll be grateful to return to the peace and tranquillity of your potting shed, even if the hairs on the back of your neck stand on end every time the door creaks open.

But if a gentler, more pastoral read will put you in the mood, I can recommend nothing better than PG Wodehouse's Blandings Castle novels. With Lord Emsworth for company you can while away the hours in a Shropshire idyll as he wrestles with his head gardener, Angus McAllister, and scratches the back of his black Berkshire sow, the Empress of Blandings, in her sty.

Ah, yes. That's the solution. Unless, of course, you fancy keeping a pig yourself. As hobbies go, there can be few that are more complementary to gardening: a pig brings relaxation when you look at it, soil cultivation courtesy of its foraging snout, and an abundant supply of manure. Keep a few chickens as well and you are set up for life. There is, after all, no better way of starting the gardening day than with a plate of bacon and eggs. There you are. Sorted.

2007

I'm Dreaming of a White-Spotted Christmas

Ghosts of Christmas past always raise their heads at this time of year. Gazing into the flames of the log fire, I can recall the Christmases past, none more vividly than when I worked in the Parks Department nursery.

Winters were definitely colder then, but we had little to warm us other than a donkey jacket and manual labour, and a couple of tatty old brown gabardine macs that hung on the back of the potting shed door, to be put over our jackets as protective clothing when we whitewashed the brick walls inside the greenhouses.

The heating would be turned off in the interests of economy, the plants having been moved out while this winter cleansing operation took place. Singing carols to myself, the better to put me in the festive spirit, I would dip the heavy, lumpen brush into the thick white Snowcem and smear it on the low brick walls that supported the staging. My voice would echo round the empty glass cathedral, the notes punctuated by the steady drip, drip of water into the massive sunken tanks into which we dipped our watering cans when the greenhouse was full of ferns or hydrangeas, pelargoniums or chrysanthemums. Two hours of this coarse artistry would build up an appetite and a thirst, to be sated with two fresh pies from the local pork butcher and a pint pot of sweet PG

Tips. Then, with a white-spotted face, I'd take up my brush once more and *Hark the herald* my way along the brickwork until dinner time. Back then, in Yorkshire we had nothing so smart as lunch.

Once a week, we'd replenish the floral displays in the troughs at the town hall. It was a simple matter to remove the fading plants and replace them with fresh ones – Indian azaleas or cinerarias at Christmas, along with fluffy green ferns for infill. I'd slip in the new plants, carefully arranging their leaves so that they looked as if they'd been growing in this most unlikely of spots all their lives. I would then stand back to admire my work, regularly tumbling down the first few steps. I soon perfected the technique of admiring them sideways on.

The *pièce de résistance* of our Christmas show was a hanging basket planted up with Christmas cacti. *Zygocactus truncatus* was one of the first Latin names I learned. It grieved me, rather, when they decided to change it to *Schlumbergera x buckleyi*, which had nothing like the festive ring to it. Nobody quite knew when this basket had first been planted up – its origins were lost in the mists of Parks Department time. But in the mid-Sixties it was fully four feet across and two feet high and it obligingly came into spectacular bloom every year in December.

We'd carry it up to the town hall, dripping vivid cerise flowers all around the back of the council van. Ron, the propagator, would be driving, and I'd be balancing the basket on top of a bucket – the only way the flower-filled stems could be protected from damage on the 10-minute journey. Once there, the wrought-iron stand kept solely for the purpose would be erected outside the secretaries' office and the basket lifted into place, to gasps of amazement from the girls, who left their typewriters to admire our handiwork. Then it was back to the nursery for more painting.

The dozen or so men who worked at the nursery would gradually enter into the Christmas spirit – coming back with things they'd nipped into the shops to buy for their wives. As Christmas Day drew nearer, so their relief at having found something suitable would be more palpable – a purse or a vanity case, a pair of gloves or a soft scarf. Only Harry B. would buy something more exotic. Lingerie. We were never allowed to see it. His wife was referred to as "the golden voice". She was small, pretty, and my youthful imagination worked over-time wondering what could be in the highly decorated 'Lucy Gray' bag that Harry B. stowed away until home time.

Harry H., on the other hand, had more pressing things on his mind – Christmas dinner. I don't know where it came from, or how he got it back to the nursery, but I can see him now, walking into the potting shed with a huge white goose under his arm. Three times it tried to escape, flapping wildly with Harry H. hanging onto its feet like something out of *Peter Pan*. Every time it was recaptured, the goose looked nervously for a means of escape – as well it might – for within the hour, Harry H. was plucking it and soft white feathers filled the potting shed like snow.

We had a white Christmas that year. Not just because it snowed, but also because the air was filled with goose feathers and my face was spattered with the distemper that gave a dozen old greenhouses a new lease of life.

I walked home at five o'clock the night before Christmas Eve. Through the falling snow I could see headlights reflected on the glistening streets and hear the swish of cars brave enough to come out on a night such as this. I'd worked at

the Parks Department for two years and wondered whether I
would spend the rest of my working life in those greenhouses.
I had simply no idea what the future held ... Ah me! Merry
Christmas!

2008

Acknowledgements

I am enormously grateful to Adam Pasco for having the nerve to let me grace the pages of *BBC Gardeners' World Magazine* with these ramblings since the magazine first saw the light of day twenty years ago. The writing of 'Tales' has been a source of continuous pleasure for me, and I'm indebted to all those readers who continue to be engaged, irritated, infuriated, bewildered or amused by my continuous presence in the magazine over two decades. The subjects of these short pieces were what seized my interest at the time or which, in desperation, I sought to explore simply to discover what my own opinions were on a range of varied issues. Some think of gardening as a blameless and calming pursuit. It can be, but it can also be irritating, infuriating, bewildering, amusing . . . well, you get my drift. Over the years my copy has been edited by many indulgent souls, especially Lucy Hall, David Hurrion, Anne Millman and Jodie Jones. I owe them much and am happy here to register my thanks. Gardening continues to be my first love and greatest passion. To write about it is an indulgence for which I never cease to be thankful.

'Tales from Titchmarsh' was first published in the launch issue of BBC *Gardeners' World Magazine* in March 1991, and has appeared in every issue of the magazine to this day.

Gardeners' World Magazine is Britain's biggest selling gardening publication, and you can read more 'Tales from Titchmarsh' every month.